Ite
h
w

CATHERINE AND FRIENDS

First published in 2010 by
Liberties Press
Guinness Enterprise Centre | Taylor's Lane | Dublin 8
www.libertiespress.com | info@libertiespress.com | +353 (1) 415 1224

Trade enquiries to Gill and Macmillan Distribution
Hume Avenue | Park West | Dublin 12
www.gillmacmillan.ie | Tel: +353 (1) 500 9534 | Fax: +353 (1) 294 9595

Distributed in the United States by
Dufour Editions
PO Box 7 | Chester Springs | Pennsylvania | 19425

and in Australia by
James Bennett Pty Limited | InBooks
3 Narabang Way | Belrose NSW 2085

Copyright © Pat Flynn, 2010

The author has asserted his moral rights.

ISBN: 978–1–905483–92–1
2 4 6 8 10 9 7 5 3

A CIP record for this title is available from the British Library
Cover design by Ros Murphy
Internal design by Liberties Press
Printed in Ireland by Colour Books

CATHERINE AND FRIENDS

PAT FLYNN

CONTENTS

1

THE PHONE CALL

It had been a good St Patrick's weekend. I was the garda super-intendent with responsibility for Gorey Garda District, County Wexford, and I was not on call that particular weekend. I was also looking forward to a holiday in Sicily, with my girlfriend. As I was getting into bed, I glanced at the alarm clock and telephone on the bedside locker. No need to set the alarm this time: a lie-in was very much on the cards. The telephone was a different kettle of fish: that would never be taken off the hook, day or night. I was awak-ened from a deep sleep by the sound of the phone ringing, and glanced apprehensively at the alarm clock, which indicated it was 4.45 AM. Past experience would suggest that this was trouble.

Garda Tony Ryan, of Arklow Garda Station, was on the phone. 'Superintendent Flynn, you had better get up to Jack White's straight away. Tom Nevin has been shot, and Catherine was tied up.' Is he dead? I enquired. Yes, came the quick reply. My usual standard of dress, be it uniform or civilian attire (consisting of a neat suit or, alternatively, a sports jacket and slacks), seemed of little importance, so I slipped quickly into a white pullover and slacks, and set out from Gorey to Jack White's pub, in Arklow, County Wicklow, a distance of seventeen miles.

En route to Jack White's Inn, I tried to grasp the magnitude of Garda Ryan's message – that a murder had been committed within the garda district for which I had responsibility. A murder, and its subsequent investigation, is not a welcome visitor to any garda superintendent, especially one in charge of a country district. With luck, a country garda superintendent might expect a murder-free tenure. I was not one of the lucky ones: this would be my third murder investigation in the space of a few years. Neither of the others had aroused such national, and even international, interest as did the murder of Tom Nevin. One was committed during a weekend motorcycle rally, and the other involved a domestic dispute in which a son was convicted of the murder of his father.

I instinctively knew that this investigation would be a minefield. Catherine Nevin, the wife of the murdered man, had crossed swords with many of the local Gardaí, and had made serious allegations against Gardaí Vincent Whelan and Michael Murphy. Not surprisingly, relations between Catherine and some Arklow-based Gardaí was little short of poisonous. However, the situation with regard to some high-ranking officers in An Garda Síochána was entirely different. She regarded some of those, especially former Inspector Tom Kennedy, as very good friends of hers.

When Catherine and Tom Nevin first took possession of Jack White's Inn, relations between them and the local Gardaí could not have been better. It was known as a 'Garda house' – at least until Catherine threw a cat among the pigeons with her complaints. This was the situation I knew awaited me on 19 March 1996. Adding to Catherine's distrust of the local Gardaí was her distrust of myself. She had unsuccessfully tried to get me on side with drink and meals (not to mention gifts of shellfish), but all to no avail.

There was a noticeable Garda presence and an ambulance outside Jack White's pub when I arrived. Gardaí Martin McAndrew and Paul Cummiskey, who were the first Gardaí to arrive at the scene, met me on arrival. A quick look at the front exterior of the premises didn't reveal any noticeable signs of a forced entry. I noticed that the front hall door was slightly ajar, and was informed by Garda McAndrew that it was in the same position then as when they had arrived at the scene. Perhaps entry, or indeed exit, by those responsible was via this door.

The sounds of a woman moaning were clearly audible. I entered and saw Catherine Nevin in a room just off the hall. Her attitude was certainly not what I had expected from a woman who had undergone an ordeal. First, she just stared at me with a contemptuous look. Aware of Catherine's feelings towards me, there wasn't any point in trying to engage her in conversation. I sympathised with her, and asked if I could be of any assistance. She continued to stare at me, and did not reply.

There was something surreal about Catherine's behaviour, which had nothing to do with her obvious distrust of me. She was displaying no emotions or grief, and was certainly not in shock. Most strikingly, there was no visible indication that this was a woman who was shattered by the murder of her beloved husband. After some minutes, it was obvious that my presence was irritating rather than helping Catherine, so I left her in the company of Detective Joe Collins.

Another example of Catherine's strange behaviour was her later request to be given a phone, as she wished to make an urgent phone call. She was not permitted to use any of the phones available on the premises until the technical examination had been completed. She shouted: 'Get me a phone, get me a fucking phone, now, at once, do you understand?' She was given a phone and made her call.

Gardaí McAndrews and Cummiskey described the scene when they arrived at 4.45 AM: Cummiskey noticed a light on in a window at the gable end of the pub – Catherine's bedroom. A light was also on in the hallway. The front door leading into the hall was slightly open. The latch on this door was in the normal position, suggesting that if the door had been pulled, it would have closed.

Both Gardaí saw Catherine behind the hall door, sitting on the ground with her hands tied behind her back. She was wearing a purple-coloured silk nightshirt and white panties. In a low, barely audible voice, she said: 'He came into the bedroom. He had a knife, and a hood over his head.' Without any effort, McAndrew released a blue dressing-gown belt tied around Catherine's wrists. Much more difficult to remove were coloured cloth headbands, also tied around her wrists. Cummiskey got a knife and cut the ties. He noticed red marks on her wrists when they were removed. There was also a nylon stocking hanging loosely around her neck, and this had been holding a pair of black panties that had been used as a gag.

Having made his way to Catherine's bedroom, Cummiskey noticed that the main ceiling light was on. The phone on the bedside locker was off the hook and the receiver was on the ground. There was a glass containing what appeared to be spirits on the floor beside the bed. The bedroom was untidy, with items of clothing and books of varying descriptions scattered about. The room, according to the staff, always looked untidy. Outside on the landing was a black portable TV, resting against the banister.

At no stage when I was present did Catherine enquire from either Garda as to the whereabouts of Tom. This, I thought, was rather strange.

On entering the kitchen area, the Gardaí saw the body of Tom Nevin, lying on his back. It was then 4.50 AM and, having found no pulse, they presumed that Tom was dead – a fact later confirmed by Dr Nicholas Buggle of Arklow. They kept the scene intact for expert examination.

Anxious to elicit any useful information, Cummiskey resumed conversation with Catherine, and asked her if she could give a description of her attackers. She was adamant that there had been only one. Catherine told McAndrews: 'The man that tied me up said "Where's the jewellery?" several times.'

Having a clearer picture, I carried out a preliminary examination of the area, concentrating on the main building and outhouses. There was no evidence of a forced entry, as all windows and doors were intact. This was difficult for me to comprehend at that early stage. If there had been no forced entry, then the intruder (or intruders) would have to have been either concealed on the premises prior to the murder, or admitted by someone after the pub had been secured at closing time.

I visited the kitchen where Tom's body was lying. Immediately of interest to me was the fact that Tom's glasses were resting on his nose in the reading position, and a biro was clasped between the fingers of his right hand. He was lying on his back with his feet facing the door, and a stool was lying upturned beside his left leg. A pool of blood was visible under the body's right side. He was wearing a dark blue jacket, dark grey slacks, and a multicoloured jumper.

On the counter close to where the body lay were cheques, receipt books and three metal tins from the floor safe. There was no evidence of a fight or struggle, and no signs of any disturbance or ransacking in or around the kitchen, bar or lounge – indeed anywhere in the entire ground-floor area. There were notes and coins – apparently untouched – in each of the three tills.

Catherine's bedroom is a large room. The couple hadn't slept in the same bedroom for years. The main centre light was on. Beside the bed, I saw a copy of the *Sunday Independent*. Prescription drugs in large quantities were noticeable on the bedside locker, and beside it was a half-full glass, containing what looked like wine. Opposite the entrance door was a chest of drawers. Three of the five drawers had been removed and were lying on the floor, with some of the contents disturbed.

Having entered Catherine's bedroom – the only one the intruders had entered, it transpired – I was amazed at what I saw. Catherine had told the Gardaí on their arrival: 'The robbers were looking for jewellery, and had threatened to kill her if they didn't get it.' If the intruders had attempted to give an impression that her room had been systematically and thoroughly searched, they failed miserably. The room was certainly untidy and unkept, but if the room had been gone over thoroughly by the intruders, it would have looked like a rubbish heap. I felt that if ever there was a contrived scene, this was it. There was a noticeable – perhaps too noticeable – presence of jewellery strewn around the landing, on the stairs, and in the lounge and bar. Also noticed in the lounge was a brown varnished jewellery box lying on the floor.

I kept asking myself: 'Why commit murder in an intended act of robbery having as its objective jewellery, and then leave without it?' There was no logic to it, other than the fact that the intruders were surprised – or, more likely, that Catherine did not want her jewellery taken in what she evidently hoped would be perceived as a botched robbery.

Detective Garda Joe Collins and Detective Garda Jim McCawl, of Arklow, were amongst the first Gardaí to arrive at the scene. They both spoke to Catherine on their arrival. Collins and Catherine, having previously enjoyed a good rapport, had a lengthy conversation. The brevity of the conversation between Catherine and Detective McCawl was due to the fact that if there was a member of An Garda Síochána that she disliked and distrusted more than me, it was McCawl.

They attempted to ascertain what had occurred earlier that morning. The interview lasted from 5.55 AM to 8 AM. Detective McCawl was present until 6.20 AM. Arising from this interview, the first taken and recorded in writing, were many interesting issues. To quote Catherine's account of events from Joe Collins's notes:

> Did the cash and went to bed about 12.30 AM. Put pillow over head. One man with a knife. He'd something woolly on his head and face, was looking for jewellery. Someone shouted and I heard a noise like a saucepan falling.
>
> There was another fellow throwing things around. He tied my hands and put something on my feet and mouth.

Got feet loose and came downstairs and pressed panic button. Tom did lodgement. Busy weekend, the amount is in the books. Is the money taken. He kept saying where is the jewellery. I told him it was in the press. I don't know if he took it all.

We have a gun. Tom has it hidden in the store, bought it from Tommy Godkin. I don't know what time it happened. Tom's mother is very old, I want to see him. Is he really dead? Two cars drove off. He told me he was going to kill me. More local accent, not Dublin accent.

Girls went to disco in bus.

Tied feet and hands with I don't know what, it took only a couple of minutes, he just tied me up so quick. I didn't see anybody except the fellow that tied me up. He woke me out of my sleep. I don't know how long I was asleep when he woke me up.

I want to see Tom before I go to hospital. He's not dead I know he's not. I pressed panic button when I got my legs free; it's at the front door.

The front door was open when I came downstairs, I tried to catch my nails in it to open it, but I couldn't, it wasn't fully open just barely.

Tom went to the bank on Friday. I went to Dr Pippet that day. Did you see him, did he suffer? Why did they do it if they got the money? I don't know how much cash there was, I only did the day's take.

None of the staff stay late on a Sunday night on bank holiday weekends, they don't go out on a Sunday night, they go out on the Monday night instead and they don't come back to stay.

The man in the bedroom had a knife; he said, "Where is the fucking jewellery?" He held my head down on the pillow, then I heard a loud noise like a big saucepan dropping. I let Dominic [Sergeant Dominic McElligott, Avoca] out, he was the last out. Tom drove Johnny Brennan home and the only other person left was Dominic McElligot.

I did tills last night, put money in the canisters and put them in the safe in the ground, the round one. I didn't make up the lodgement. Tom always does that, he doesn't like anybody else doing it. Tom did the lodgement last night in the kitchen.

I was tied up for a long time. My ankles were tied to my hands for a long time. I got the legs free. I got the receiver off the phone and tried to dial 999.

All my jewellery in case. Tom may have had some in the safe downstairs. I told the ones that the jewellery was in the press in the room. Someone shouted downstairs when I heard the loud bang like a saucepan falling.

Tom came back after a short time and Dominic left. I let him out. I went to bed when Dominic left. I was in bed by half twelve.

I hid our gun in the bedroom but Tom brought it downstairs as he thought it too dangerous. I have cartridges in my bedroom and Tom has some. It's up in the rafters in the store. I am the licence holder.

Tom never has less than £500 in his wallet. He [the intruder] seemed big, aggressive; I thought he was going to kill me. He put something to my back; I just saw a blade, a small blade. He never looked for money. About £400 in my handbag, everything in the safe. Tom was followed on several occasions on returning from Dublin.

The significance and importance of the notes taken during this interview cannot be overstated. As the investigation progressed, many of Catherine's utterances would come to be seen as bare-faced lies. When recounting events later to other people, she would contradict her version of events as given that morning.

Detective Collins and Detective Sergeant Fergus O'Brien, of

Wicklow, returned to Jack White's Inn later that day to take a written statement from Catherine Nevin. Her attitude to this reasonable request was amazing: 'I gave you a statement today.' Collins informed her that what he had taken earlier that day was notes regarding her account of events. What he now wanted was to get this in the form of a written statement. She replied: 'I will make no statement or sign anything. It's dangerous to sign statements, I know. I want a guarantee from a superior officer – and not from Superintendent Flynn, because I don't trust him – that my statement won't turn up on the desk in Arklow, to have it doctored, the same as the other statement. I don't trust anybody in Arklow station – present company excluded.'

On the advice of her solicitor, she eventually relented, and made a statement on 20 March 1996. During this meeting, Collins showed her the jewellery box and the jewellery which had been found scattered around the premises the morning of the murder. She agreed that both the box and the jewellery were hers, and stated: 'None of my jewellery was taken in the raid.' Other interviews would follow; O'Brien and Collins were chosen to carry out these – and indeed all other contacts between Catherine and the Gardaí.

After the funeral of Tom Nevin, a large number of people returned to the pub. They were joined by O'Brien and Collins. At about 10 PM on that day, 21 March, Catherine told them that on the morning of the murder, after she had let Sergeant Dominic McElligott out the hall door, she pushed the door closed; it Yale-locked, and then she mortise-locked it by turning the Chubb key. She then hung the key on the wall beside the door. In her earlier statement, she had said: 'The Sergeant had just pulled the door behind him and it Yale-locked.' She had made no mention of mortise-locking it.

She also told the two detectives that when she was trying to release herself after the intruders had left her bedroom, she got an unusual smell, as though the place was on fire. This had the detectives puzzled. Later, they would realise that she had hoped that the smell would be accepted as that emanating after a gun had been fired. Unfortunately for her, expert evidence would prove that she could not have got such a smell coming from the kitchen in her bedroom. The only possible way she could have got this smell was if she had been in the kitchen prior to, during, or immediately after Tom had been shot.

On 23 March, she told the Gardaí that the amount of money stolen in the raid was £16,500, made up of:

£4,500	Payment from billboards (displayed on pub premises)
£1,800	Catherine's personal cash
£2,000	Sterling
£3,000	Takings from Monday to Thursday, 11 to 14 March
£500	Takings for Friday, 15 March
£1,700	Takings for 16 March
£1,500	Takings for 17 March
£1,500	Takings for 18 March

The interviews by Fergus O'Brien and Joe Collins with Catherine Nevin revealed numerous contradictions and lies in her story, and were instrumental in casting her in the role of a very credible and likely suspect.

As I left Jack White's the morning of the murder, secure in the knowledge that there had been no interference with the scene, I could not dismiss the possibility that Catherine was a suspect. An interesting visitor to the pub that morning was former garda inspector Tom Kennedy. I had known him and, out of curiosity as to what he would say, spoke to him briefly about the murder. 'Terrible affair, Pat,' he said. 'Just heard it on the news. That poor woman, what they have done to her, such a decent honourable woman.' There was no mention of poor Tom, whose cold dead body lay just a few yards away.

On my arrival at Arklow Garda Station, an incident room was already in place. Next on the agenda was the selection of an investigation team, who would remain based at Arklow Garda Station. The investigation team includes those regarded as most efficient in investigating crimes. Invariably, the majority will be drawn from within the district where the crime was committed, with others coming from within the garda division. (Gorey is the garda district where the crime was committed, and Wexford/Wicklow is the garda division.)

The technical experts, such as Ballistics, Fingerprints, Mapping and Photography, are provided from Garda Headquarters on request by the officer in charge. Their presence is limited to examining the scene, reporting on their findings and giving evidence in court.

At 9 AM, members of the investigation team began to arrive at Arklow Garda Station. Detective Superintendent John McElligot, of Garda Headquarters, arrived; he would have a continuous presence throughout the investigation. He is acknowledged as one of the best in the force at coordinating and analysing the progress of serious-crime investigations.

Detective Bernie Hanley, of the Serious Crime Investigations Unit, was well known as an outstanding investigator and interrogator. He had been involved in practically every major crime investigation in the state for many years. Being of a rather quiet disposition and a friendly personality, he would be a pleasure to work with.

Liam Hogan, also of the Serious Crime Investigations Unit, held the rank of detective sergeant. (At this time, his unquestionable talents, and intelligence, in all aspects of police work had not been properly acknowledged. Gladly, this situation has to an extent been rectified, as he now holds the rank of superintendent.) Hogan's expertise includes the examination of statements, documents and so on, and file preparation. He would take responsibility for the paper side of the investigation. His task was enormous, and essential to the final outcome of the investigation.

Liam would be ably assisted by Detective Aubrey Steedman. Every investigation team needs at least one personality such as Aubrey. His happy-go-lucky attitude is infectious, and of great help during an occasional hiccup or tense moment.

On the local front, Arklow would supply the bulk of the investigation team. These included Detective Gardaí Joe Collins, Jim McCawl and Tom Byrne, and Gardaí Paul Cummiskey, Liam O'Gorman, Martin Kavanagh, Martin McAndrew and Donal O'Leary. Sergeant Brian Duffy completed the Arklow contingent. Gorey was represented by Sergeant Joe O'Hara, Detective Gerry McKenna and Garda Joe O'Sullivan. Wexford Garda Station supplied Detective Pat Mulcahy and Wicklow Detective Sergeant Fergus O'Brien.

As I glanced around the table in the incident room at the assembled investigation team, I thought: if there is a possibility that this crime can be solved, then these are the men capable of doing it.

2

THE INVESTIGATION COMMENCES

Some minutes into the first conference with the investigation team, I got a phone call from my girlfriend, asking the dreaded question: 'Pat, are we still going on holidays tomorrow?' Thankfully, she appreciated my position. The investigation would take precedence – except for urgent family considerations and demands. Leave would not be granted other than for exceptional reasons.

The media was the next subject to be addressed. I told the team that leaks to the media would not under any circumstances be tolerated. Should there be any deviation from this instruction, and the identity of the individual was discovered, I would recommend that person's instant dismissal.

At 12.30 PM, Tom McCaughren of RTÉ requested an interview about the murder for the 1 PM news. Conscious of my attire – Bainín pullover, shirt and slacks, rather than uniform – I told Tom that my clothes might not be ideal. Tom informed me that Assistant Commissioner Jim McHugh had nominated me to do the interview. As we had spoken earlier and he was aware of my attire, I went ahead and did the interview. I was pleasantly surprised later to receive a number of letters praising my efforts –

with some even complimenting me on my less-than-formal clothing!

Not so welcome was an official letter from Assistant Commissioner Pat Byrne, later to become garda commissioner, received a few days after the interview. It commenced by congratulating me on the content of the interview. However, my choice of dress was not to Byrne's liking. How embarrassing it must have been for him to see an officer of 'his force', as he liked to refer to An Garda Síochána, appear on television other than like a dressed dummy.

On the arrival of the Dublin-based members – Bernie Hanley, Liam Hogan and Aubrey Steedman – one of the local detectives was heard to refer to them with venom as 'The Amigos'. Hogan and Hanley had been chosen to investigate Nevin's serious allegations against Gardaí Vincent Whelan and Michael Murphy, both of whom had been suspended from duty. They were treated like suspected criminals. (Murphy and Whelan were cleared of allegations by the DPP, who directed that no criminal proceedings should be taken against either Garda. They were both restored to full operational duties: Garda Murphy was appointed to the traffic corps based in Gorey, where he is still employed; Garda Whelan was appointed to Detective Branch in Arklow, where he is still employed.)

Liam Hogan and Bernie Hanley did not relish that investigation, but they did not have the option of passing the poisoned chalice. Convincing the local Gardaí of their bona fides was not difficult, and 'The Amigos' became Bernie and Liam once more. A friendly and creative working atmosphere was established, and this would continue for the duration of the investigation.

There is an acceptable and basic rule when it comes to murder investigations: as time passes in each case, the chances of solving it lessen. If there is not an early outcome, then the investigation will become prolonged and more difficult with each day's passing.

Police authorities hope for, and expect, an early result – and for obvious reasons. Members engaged on such investigations are usually the pick of the crop from within the local division, and are augmented by technical experts. However, officers allocating local members to a particular case will be mindful of the drain on available manpower, not to mention overtime expenditure.

During the first conference, all were in agreement that what had taken place at Jack White's pub was not a robbery, and that Catherine Nevin could, even at that early stage, be regarded as a suspect. Her story simply did not ring true. The question could be asked as to whether the detectives made the mistake of investigating Catherine rather than the crime (known in police circles as 'suspect-of-convenience syndrome'). The answer is a simple no: her demeanour, aggressiveness, lies and lack of cooperation had placed this suspicion firmly in the minds of the detectives. There were suspects thrown into the ring by Catherine; all were investigated. Needless to say, all of her accusations and theories turned out to be 'pie in the sky'.

3

THE TECHNICAL INVESTIGATION

Garda experts from the Technical Bureau arrived throughout 19 March and began their investigations, which continued well into the next day. Catherine remained at the pub throughout, despite being advised to leave and seek hospital care for the aches and pains of which she was complaining. Her raucous behaviour was causing a great deal of annoyance, as the Gardaí examining the scene did not want any distractions.

Detective Garda William Brennan, Ballistics, at that time had eighteen years' experience in the examination and testing of firearms and ammunition, in the examination of scenes of serious crimes, and in the subsequent giving of evidence in court. The report on his findings was eagerly awaited, and disclosed many interesting facts.

He described the main building as a very large, three-storey construction, used as a private dwelling, with a small portion at the right rear used as a hairdressing salon. To the left was a two-storey building adjoining the main building. The top floor was for private use, and the ground floor contained a number of interlinked bars and lounge areas. At the rear were a number of single-storey buildings, in which were housed various function rooms, a dining conservatory, the kitchen, store rooms, and the toilets. It was possible to access all areas of the entire premises internally. The only entrance door which was not locked was the front entrance door to the main building. Most of the windows and the rearmost doors appeared not to have been opened for some time.

The buildings were protected by a burglar alarm system, which had been installed and was maintained by DJ Alarms. The system had four external alarm boxes, and a panic attack alarm linked directly to a twenty-four-hour monitoring station in Dublin. The panic alarm could be triggered by pressing any one of five push buttons located throughout the premises, and two radio remote buttons. One of the fixed panic buttons was located on the frame of the front door, beside a curtain. This button had been pressed and not reset. Alan Fitzsimons from DJ Alarms confirmed that the alarm, and all the triggering devices, were working properly. Fitzsimons also stated that the last alarm activation had been triggered by the panic attack button behind the front door.

Detective Brennan noticed a night latch lock and a mortise lock fitted on the front door of the main house. He found no evidence of a forced entry.

He saw that the kitchen door was open, and noted that there was neither a door handle or a lock body fitted to it. On the lino-covered floor he saw the body of a male, who was identified to him as Tom Nevin. The dead man was lying on his back with his feet facing towards the door, with both arms outstretched. A metal stool was close to the deceased's left leg.

A large pool of blood was visible under the right side of the body. He also noted heavy bloodstains on the left hand. Tom Nevin was wearing glasses, which were undisturbed, and held a red-and-white-coloured biro pen, clenched tightly under his right index finger.

There was a large wound on the right side of the chest which looked like a shotgun entry wound. There were also portions of what appeared to be fibre shotgun wads (a cotton wool-type substance which is packed into shotgun cartridges), and white polystyrene granules on the outer surface of the jacket. A black leather wallet was lying on the top of the right inside pocket, and the pocket was badly torn. As the wound was not in line with the pocket, the removal of the wallet and the damage to the pocket appeared to have been done afterwards. The contents of the wallet appeared to have been undisturbed.

On the counter close to where the body was lying, he saw more small fragments of fibre shotgun wads and white polystyrene granules. On the counter was a half-pint drinking glass containing a small amount of stout.

He located a small wall safe which was concealed over the top shelf of the store, in which were two antique cluster rings and an antique gold bracelet. These were later identified as being Catherine's.

Catherine gave him permission to have her face and hands swabbed for firearms residue, though she told him that she had already washed her hands.

Later that day, Brennan attended the post-mortem examination at Wicklow Hospital Morgue, performed by Professor J. F. Harbison. He noted that the hole in Tom Nevin's shirt measured one and a half inches by one and three-eighths inches. Professor Harbison took X-rays of the deceased's upper chest area; these showed that there were four large-gauge lead pellets lodged in the left chest area of the deceased. The pellets had entered through the right chest area, passed through his heart, causing massive injury, and contined into the left armpit area, in a straight upwards trajectory.

The following day, in additon to what he had already observed, Brennan took note of further relevant evidence. He saw no sign of any disturbance and ransacking in any of the ground-floor rooms, including the lounge, bar and kitchen areas. The cash tills were all open, and a float of about £80, in notes and coins, in each was untouched.

On a small wooden table on the landing of the stairs, leading up from the front door, was a white telephone, and the handset had been removed from the cradle. The phone was working, and there was an engaged tone from it. A portable TV was lying against the banister just outside Catherine's bedroom, and one of the wooden rails beside it was freshly broken.

In Catherine's bedroom there were two small table lamps located on wooden bedside lockers at each side of the double bed, and these were turned off. There was a telephone on one of the bedside lockers, and the handset had been removed and placed on top of the underwear on the carpet beside it. Other items on, and in, the locker were undisturbed.

On the right side of the bed, the door of the bedside locker was open, and a large amount of prescription drugs, both inside and on the top, were undisturbed. Also beside the locker was a black ladies' handbag, the contents of which were lying on the carpet. The contents included a bank deposit book, a brown purse, bank cards, a small amount of coins, and some documents.

Also, there was a low octagonal table in the area, and fixed underneath it he found a panic attack button unit. On the windowsill behind the right side of the bed he saw a second unit. Both had a battery attached and appeared to be functioning. These units are designed to be carried on the person and intended to activate the alarm system from anywhere in or around the immediate area of the premises.

A box of twenty-five twelve-gauge express 'pro one ounce competition' type, number seven and a half shot-size shotgun cartridges were on the windowsill behind the bed.

On 29 March 1996, Brennan received from Detective John O'Neill a twelve-gauge BSA single-barrel trench-loading shotgun. This was the same shotgun he had seen at Jack White's pub, and was registered to Catherine. It had not been discharged recently, and was eliminated as the murder weapon.

On 4 April, Brennan and other members of the investigation team met at Jack White's pub to carry out tests in the kitchen. This was to establish the veracity of Catherine's description of the noise she heard coming from downstairs. Brennan had two single-barrel shotguns (one was a sawn-off shotgun) and live rounds of ammunition. There are two doors between the lounges and the private part of the premises. Different combinations were used during the tests: i.e. one door left open, two doors open, and both doors closed.

It was only possible to recover two of the four visible pellets from the deceased's body. They were of S.G. shot size used to bring down big game such as deer. The white polystyrene granules found on the deceased's jacket and jumper are used in the packing of these types of heavy shotgun cartridges. Detective Brennan used CLEY shotgun cartridges, which contains a modern nitro-cellulose-lased propellant powder, designed to produce low levels of smoke and odour. He discharged six cartridges during the tests.

Catherine had given permission for the tests to be carried out on the premises, but would not under any circumstances allow any Garda to position himself in her bedroom, the door of which she kept locked. It was imperative to re-enact Catherine's story about the noise she had heard and the smell she got in her bedroom during the robbery.

Detective Superintendent John McElligot positioned himself in the bedroom beside Catherine's. He stated: 'The first shot sounded like a telephone directory being dropped on a concrete floor. The second was somewhat louder. Neither was recognisable as a gunshot. The third and fourth were recognised as gunshots.' Shot five he compared with shot number two, and shot six to shot number one. From the bedroom, he could hear the two detectives talking in the kitchen. On completion of the tests, he went immediately to the kitchen, where he got a mild smell of firearm residue.

Detective Garda John O'Neill, Fingerprint Section, Garda Technical Bureau, examined the murder scene on 20 March. In the public lounge, he developed finger- and palm-prints from a jewellery box and its contents, which were lying on the floor. It transpired that these prints were Catherine's; no other prints or marks were found on the box or the contents.

Having obtained Catherine's permission, he examined her bedroom, which was noticeably disturbed. Boxes used for storing goods, such as bedding, were removed from the wardrobe. The impression he got was that these boxes had been knocked out of the wardrobe, rather than systematically removed and searched. He developed marks which gave him the impression that the hands which removed them had been wearing either surgical or fine leather gloves. This was a direct reference to the drawers which had been removed from the chest of drawers. The marks had definitely not been made by bare hands.

He examined the Nevins' family car, a black Opel Omega, which had been recovered the day after the murder at Dartmouth Square, Dublin. It had been missing, presumably stolen as a getaway car.

Another fingerprint expert, and a man with vast experience, Detective Sergeant Moses Morrissey, noted that Catherine's bedroom did not show signs of having been greatly disturbed. Neither did the drawers laid out on the floor, or the overturned cardboard boxes which were in the bottom of the press.

John McCullough, forensic scientist at the Forensic Science Laboratory, Garda Headquarters, Dublin, received a total of ninety-two exhibits of a diverse nature for testing. His report supplied the following information.

Tom Nevin's jacket, jumper, shirt, vest and trousers were extensively bloodstained. There was a single hole in the right side of the chest area of the jacket, and two holes in the left shoulder-blade area, with corresponding damage to the jumper, shirt and vest. The right hand inside pocket of the jacket was missing, and appeared to have been torn out. The lining on the inside breast pocket, the outside left-hand pocket, and the inside left-hand pocket, had been pulled inside out. There were two keys in the outside right-hand pocket of the jacket.

The jacket had a number of small fragments of white material on the surface, which McCullough analysed and found to be polyethylene. This is a compound used in the construction of certain shotgun cartridges.

The pocket he received from Detective John O'Neill was of similar dimensions to the torn portion inside the right front of Tom Nevin's jacket. The wallet fitted snugly into this pocket, extending out at the top of the pocket so as to be clearly visible.

A comparison of the relevant position of the holes in Tom Nevin's jacket, and his jumper and shirt, suggested that his jacket was open at the time he was shot. The edge of the right lapel of the jacket was damaged by the shot but the inside right-hand pocket area was not.

The firearms discharge residue kit used to sample the face and hands of Catherine Nevin for particles of firearms discharge residue was examined by Brennan, with negative results. However, he noted that these samples were not taken until more than eleven hours after the probable time of the shooting. Her nightdress and cardigan gave similar results. Her clothing contained no visible blood stains.

Dr Mary Casey, forensic scientist at the Forensic Science Laboratory, carried out tests on a blood and urine sample from Tom Nevin, revealing that the blood contained 119 milligrams of ethanol per 100 millitres and the urine contained 129 milligrams of ethanol per 100 millitres.

The chain of command in the South Eastern Region at the time of the murder was: Assistant Commissioner J. McHugh, in charge of the region; Chief Superintendent M. Murphy, in charge of the Wexford Division; and myself, in charge of the Gorey District.

On the morning of the murder, Assistant Commissioner McHugh's observations were the same as those of the other Garda experts. However, he was struck by the fact that the raiders had even contemplated stealing the portable TV set which was lying beside the banister outside Catherine's bedroom.

Speaking to Catherine, he thought that she appeared to be in shock and traumatised. She told him that, at about 12.10 AM, Tom drove two elderly customers home; he returned about fifteen minutes later. The only customer remaining at that time was Sergeant Dominic McElligott. He left; she walked with him to the door, and closed it after him. Tom was tidying up in the bar. She told him that she was going to bed, and took a glass of Scotch with her. She read for a short while and fell asleep.

Suddenly she was awakened by a masked man pushing her head into a pillow. He had a knife and kept repeating: 'Where's the fucking jewellery?' She was conscious of a second person being in the room but didn't see him. Her hands were tied behind her back, and her feet were drawn upwards in a backward movement towards her hands, and her legs tied at her ankles. Something was stuffed into her mouth, and something was tied over her mouth and knotted behind her head. As all this was happening, she heard a noise from downstairs, like a saucepan falling on the floor.

She tried to dial 999; but her hands were still tied behind her back, and the receiver fell on the floor. Eventually she got downstairs, and noticed the front door slightly open. She tried to open it fully but couldn't. She succeeded in pressing the panic button in the hall behind the front door. She remained there until the arrival of the Gardaí.

When Assistant Commissioner McHugh asked her if it had not, during her horrific ordeal, occurred to her to look for her husband, or call out his name, she replied: 'For whatever reason it never entered my mind. It was only when Gardaí McAndrew and

Cummiskey arrived, and asked where is Tom, that it entered my mind.' She said that Tom slept in a separate bedroom, in the old part of the building. She asked to see Tom's body, but was told that as it was a murder scene, it couldn't be interfered with.

On 23 March, McHugh, with Detective Bernie Hanley, again spoke to Catherine at the pub. She claimed that Tom was a chain smoker, smoking about sixty a day, and that he drank about a litre of whiskey each day. A few days later, Catherine asked McHugh to meet her at the pub. On this occasion, she mentioned the complaints she had made against local Gardaí and the previous investigation by Gardaí. She also said that she was not involved in any extra-marital relationships: she had many male friends but she wasn't intimately involved with any of them.

Her request to see McHugh was typical of her attitude towards authority and officialdom: get them on side if possible – and the higher-up they were, the better. She failed with McHugh. Later, in conversation with one of the investigation team, she commented: 'That dickhead. I don't know how they ever made him an assistant commissioner.'

On 3 April, she told McHugh that when she was at Tom's funeral mass, she got the same smell from the burning incense she had got from the kitchen on the morning Tom was murdered.

Detective Garda Patrick Darcy is allocated to the Garda Bureau of Fraud Investigation and is a member of the Chartered Association of Certified Accountants. He examined books and records relating to the business affairs of Catherine and Tom Nevin.

One book shows what appears to be a record of daily takings for the bar and lounge of the pub. It commences on 10 February 1996, and the last entry is dated 18 March 1996. The daily takings were divided into bar (lounge 2) at the top half of each page, and for lounge 1 at the bottom half of each page. Apparently, the register receipt roll was checked at the end of each night, and closing figures for each day's takings were entered into this book. The closing figures for the previous day's takings were also entered, and the difference indicated the amount of business that had been conducted. Having checked the figures in this book against the receipt rolls, it was noted that the figures for 18 March 1996 matched.

It appears that cash floats for £50 and £80 were held daily for both areas. An additional item, 'subs', amounting to £100, is shown in the day's takings on 18 March. The total in the book for 18 March is £2,389.26.

As the last-shown transaction in the cash registers was between 0.43 AM and 0.56 AM, it is reasonable to assume that the murder of Tom Nevin happened after 0.56 AM.

The post-mortem examination of a murder victim is obviously of immense importance. The state pathologist, Dr John Harbison, had held that position for many years. He is also professor of forensic medicine at the Royal College of Surgeons in Ireland and lecturer in medical jurisprudence at Trinity College Dublin. He is regarded by his peers as without equal in his profession.

In the kitchen, Dr Harbison saw Tom Nevin's body lying flat on his back, fully clothed, and with his jacket open. There was a hole visible in the pullover and the jacket which he was wearing over it. An equivalent hole was present in the shirt, and beneath it was an entry wound from a shotgun. He examined the left side of the chest and saw no sign of any exit. There was no satelliting (independent pellet marking around the margin of the wound). This suggested that the shot had been fired from a range of not more than a yard; perhaps two yards would be the outer limit. Certainly a shotgun shot seemed the almost certain cause of this wound. Amongst the items he noticed in the kitchen was a half-full, half-pint glass of stout.

Dr Harbison carried out the post-mortem examination in Wicklow General Hospital. He recorded an entry wound on the right exterior aspect of the chest. Two small exit wounds were visible just below the back of the left armpit on the outer side of the chest. When the body was viewed from the back, another exit wound was visible over the left shoulder blade. X-rays showed four large pellets in the soft tissues in, around and below the left shoulder joint.

There were also abrasions and bruising on the left lower shin. These would have been caused by some object striking the leg in an upwards and backwards direction, or the deceased's leg falling in a downwards and forward direction against a fixed object.

Two shot cords from a shotgun cartridge were removed from the tissues beneath the entry wound. The pellets had passed through the lung and the base of the heart, extensively lacerating the right atrium in particular and, to a lesser extent, the left one. The pulmonary trunk and ascending aorta were both severely damaged. The coronary arteries were lacerated in several places. The pellets exited through the chest walls.

Two of the projectiles were found in the blood clot in the body sheet. Two more of the pellets were located in the subcutaneous tissue, one between the scapula (shoulder blade) and the skin on the left side of the body and the other slightly below it in the muscle.

An aroma of alcoholic drink was apparent from the body: there was 129 milligrams of alcohol per 100 millilitres of urine.

Dr Harbison concluded:

> The deceased Thomas Nevin in my opinion died of acute cerebral anoxia, as a result of instant stoppage of his circulation as a result of massive gunshot injuries to his heart, aorta and pulmonary trunk. This had given rise to bilateral heamothoraces amounting to 1.75 litres in all.
>
> The deceased had been hit by a single discharge from a shotgun into the right side of the chest at the front. This had resulted in six very large lead pellets traversing his chest from the right front to the left back, and they exited from the chest cavity in the region of the left shoulder blade, two from the body altogether, and four into soft tissues around and below the right shoulder . . . . The ori-

gin of this shot from a twelve-bore cartridge was shown by the finding of two shot cords in the deceased's tissues. . . . The range of this shot, while necessitating verification by test card finding, was certainly not more then two yards and could have been less.

The deceased was said to have died between midnight and 4 AM . . . Mr Nevin was a fairly healthy man at the time of his death, though his liver showed fat infiltration suggestive of alcohol abuse.

There was no damage to Mr Nevin's spine, and therefore none to his spinal cord. Theoretically, he could have moved after being shot, and even remained standing until he lost consciousness. Thereafter, he would not have been capable of voluntary movement. There is no sign of any 'wipe' marks in the pooled blood on the floor beside the body. Therefore his body does not seem to have moved or been moved, after he fell to the floor. His right arm could, however, have been swung out, for example to gain access to the inside pocket of his jacket, after his death.

Neither the pools of blood beside the body, nor the faint stains a distance from it, suggest to me that there were signs of a struggle. This is further suggested by the presence of the deceased's glasses on his nose and a pen in his hand. Rather he appears to have been surprised, while counting his money.

With reference to his glasses and pen, however, both of these could have been placed in position on the body after death or after loss of consciousness; the glasses because he lay face up and the pen because it was not in a tight grip, i.e. with the back in cadaveric spasm or instant rigor mortis.

Technical examinations at serious-crime scenes frequently disclose significant evidence, which is of great importance in making an arrest and in any subsequent trial. The results of the tests and examinations at this particular murder scene, though not creating a positive breakthrough, nonetheless steered the investigation team in a particular direction.

4

THE FUNERAL

Tom Nevin's funeral aroused huge public interest and heartfelt sorrow for Catherine and the Nevin family. He was buried at Barndarrig graveyard, a typical rural setting. As is the custom at local funerals, the church and graveyard were thronged during the services. The attendance at Tom Nevin's funeral was far higher than anything seen previously in the locality. The media were present in huge numbers. Also noticeable were local TDs, dignitaries and Gardaí.

How grief-stricken Catherine looked, as she clutched a single red rose to her chest. Many in attendance wondered if this open and public display of grief was genuine. The huge attendance, interspersed with so many luminaries from various walks of life, perhaps represented long-sought-after recognition for her, and in her mind placed her on the pedestal she felt she deserved. The media and photographers mingling with others in the graveyard were no doubt an added incentive for her to put her beauty on display. However, the national newspapers the following day did not present things as she would have hoped.

It was also the culmination of Catherine's scheming over many years: Tom had been permanently removed, and she was now available as a woman of quality, property and wealth. The floodgates were now open, and there would be no shortage of eminent and desirable suitors. Gone forever, banished to the wilderness, were her previous lovers, none of whom could any longer be considered as either suitable or desirable.

Prior to the funeral, Catherine's attention to detail was to manifest itself. Tom's funeral suit, which Detective McCawl had got from Tom's bedroom when requested, was not to her liking. When she discovered who had chosen the suit, Catherine nearly blew a fuse, and demanded another suit, of her choosing.

Catherine was determined that a permanent and poignant reminder of the broken woman left behind would be etched in stone for posterity on Tom's headstone. Much thought no doubt went into her choice of words:

> In loving memory of Thomas (Tom) Nevin, Jack White's Inn, Brittas Bay, who was murdered on 19 March 1996, aged 54 years, Rest in Peace.
>
> When a loved one goes, those we love remain with us, for love itself lives on, and cherished memories never fade, because a loved one's gone. Those we love can never be more than a thought apart, for as long as there is memory, they'll live on in the heart.
>
> Loved ones never go away.
> Do not stand at my grave and weep,
> I am not there,
> I do not sleep,
> I am a thousand winds that blow
> I am the diamond glints on the snow
> I am the gentle autumn rain
> When you awaken in the morning hour
> I am the swift uplifting rush
> Of quiet birds in circled flight
> I am the soft stars that shine at night

Do not stand at my grave and cry
I am not there
I did not die.

The Mass card chosen by Catherine read:

There is a reason
For every pain that we must bear, for every care
There is a reason
For every grief that bows the head
For every tear that we shed
There is a reason
But if we trust in God as we should
All must work out for the good
He knows the reason.

Genuine grief was displayed by most at the funeral. Tom's immediate family were in a state of shock and disbelief as to what had happened. Many were unable to control their emotions, and sobbed pitifully. Unwelcomed as death is, it pales into significance compared with the loss through murder of a son, brother, relative and friend.

There was a noticeable coolness evident between the Nevin family and Catherine. Both sides were ill at ease in the other's company, and made little effort to hide their feelings. Catherine, it transpired, had tried to turn Tom against his family from the outset of their relationship. Her dislike of Tom's family was to manifest itself in many ways, particularly in her comments to her staff. 'Grabbers', she considered them, adding: 'Where there is a blade of grass, you would find the Nevins.' How wide of the mark she was with her description of them. The Nevins are decent, law-abiding, honourable people, and held in high esteem by all who know them.

Catherine's card had been marked by the Nevins shortly after their first meeting. They had wanted Tom to be happy and successful in life – all the more so after the breakdown of his first marriage to June O'Flanagan. The Nevins saw Catherine as a dangerous and manipulative woman, incapable of true love and affection. Was it therefore any wonder that friends and foe alike commented on the apparent coldness displayed between Catherine and Tom's family during the funeral services.

Theresa Nevin was married to Sean Nevin (since deceased), a brother of Tom's. She travelled from Galway along with other members of the family to attend Tom's funeral. On entering the pub, she saw Catherine having her hair done. Catherine jumped up and hugged Rose, a sister-in-law of Tom's. Theresa felt that Catherine was trying to cry but was putting on an act.

Catherine told them that she went to bed shortly after midnight on the night of the murder. She was almost asleep when two men burst in the door of her bedroom. She didn't see them, as they were wearing balaclavas, and one had a knife. This intruder held the knife to her throat and was shouting at the other one: 'Get the fucking jewellery.' They then tied her up.

After the funeral, Theresa went into the kitchen at the pub, where Catherine was in conversation with a man whom she introduced as Tom's bank manager. She was telling him that she had gone to bed on the night of the murder, and she was up in bed reading for a while when the door burst open. When he asked her if she had seen the raiders, Catherine said: 'It was dark.' Rose picked her up on this, and asked: 'But Catherine, if it was dark, how could you have been reading?' Catherine ignored her and went on to explain about the noise she had heard in the kitchen. Catherine also mentioned finding a pocket of Tom's jacket that the Gardaí had missed under a bench. This was the bloodstained pocket she was seen holding the day of the murder. Throughout their entire visit, Theresa felt, as did other members of the family, that Catherine showed no emotion and appeared to be in full control at all times.

After the funeral, a large number of people returned to Jack White's. Detective Sergeant O'Brien and Detective Collins met

Catherine with Tom Kennedy, a retired garda inspector. She told them that after she had left Sergeant Dominic McElligot out through the front door on 19 March, she pushed the door closed and it Yale-locked. She mortise-locked the door by turning the Chubb key, and hung the key up on the wall beside the door. However, in an earlier statement, she had said that Sergeant McElligott just pulled the door after him, and it Yale-locked. She made no mention of mortise-locking it. She also told them that when she was trying to release herself in the bedroom, she got an unusual smell, as though the place was on fire.

Catherine was trying to place firmly in the minds of the investigating Gardaí the events of 18/19 March, piece by piece. She felt that her plan had been meticulously and even professionally thought out, but she had, it seems, forgotten the old adage: 'To be a good liar one needs a good memory.' Even at this early stage, she was beginning to give different versions of the events that took place on that fateful night.

As the Nevin family left Ballynapark the morning after the funeral, they did so with heavy hearts and suspicious minds. They also brought with them an intensified distrust for Catherine, who they were fully convinced had played a significant, perhaps even a major, role in the murder of their brother Tom.

The Nevins sought my confirmation that their suspicions about Catherine were justified. The humane side of me wanted to give a positive reaction, but professionally this was impossible. They demanded an immediate and positive resolution of the case, which was understandable, given the hurt and anger they were feeling. I felt – correctly, as it transpired – that the Nevin family would be difficult to appease otherwise. Patsy Nevin, brother of Tom Nevin, was to be their spokesperson, and would on occasions test my patience. Fortunately, we remained friends throughout the investigation and trial, despite a few blips along the way.

5

CATHERINE'S SUSPECTS

Catherine was not slow in nominating some candidates whom she believed were worthy of serious consideration in relation to the murder of her husband. In her written statement, she pointed the finger of suspicion firmly at a man and woman who had stayed overnight at the pub on 26 February 1996. They had arrived the previous evening and booked bed and breakfast. They had stayed that Sunday night and again on 10 March 1996. They were given the room next to Catherine's bedroom.

The man was described by Catherine as having an athletic build and a moustache, five foot ten inches tall, a real ladies' man, a spoofer, with a cultured Dublin accent, about thirty. Money was no object to him, she said. She was about thirty and was 'well-preserved', five foot one or two, and well-endowed. She had a lot of make-up 'plastered on', and was 'really fat', not expensively dressed, and looked like someone on a limited budget. They didn't appear to be married.

His companion was drinking brandy and port, and he was drinking heavily (pints of Budweiser) but didn't get drunk. He said he owned a hair salon. 'I thought he was a bit of a liar.' He spoke to her about Tom, and enquired: 'Houses going well in

Dublin? Does Tom still go up on a Monday?'

She said: 'He made reference to my birthday cards, and was being overfamiliar with me, which wasn't right. I don't know how he knew about Tom's business. I found it a bit strange but it might not be unusual for someone to know someone who knows Tom. The woman was bottle-blonde . . . She said she had a sister in London who was hairdressing.'

Continuing her account of the two 'suspects', she said the man paid in cash for the accommodation and told her they had stayed with a friend in a mansion in Wexford, owned by someone who was home from England.

The woman had in fact known Catherine casually for eight years, but Catherine set out to give the impression that they were complete strangers to her.

This particular saga took an interesting twist when it was discovered that Catherine had refused them accommodation for 17/18 March (the night before the murder), her reason being that they were booked out. That was another falsehood – and she had in fact refused all other requests for accommodation on that particular weekend.

The man told the Gardaí that he had never mentioned Tom Nevin's business but that it was Catherine who had broached the topic. This was meant to be seen as a direct accusation that he knew about these, thus throwing suspicion on him. Catherine had previously alleged that on a number of occasions when he was returning from Dublin, Tom had been followed.

There were other suspects thrown into the ring by Catherine, and all were fully investigated. Needless to say, there was not a syllable of truth in any of her theories.

6

EVALUATION

Suspects are the lifeblood of any serious-crime investigation. Occasionally, the finger of suspicion will point towards a particular individual or individuals. The modus operandi may lead the investigation team in a particular direction, as many criminals have peculiar characteristics in the way they operate, such as how they gained entry, their target, the type of violence used, if any, and so on.

Having reviewed this particular crime, the modus operandi just didn't make sense. If the intruders wanted jewellery and were prepared, according to Catherine, to kill for it, why did they not take even one single item of jewellery? There was even ambiguity as to whether one, two or even three raiders had been involved. Catherine's life was threatened but Tom was killed for no apparent reason. There was no forced entry. Her story was packed with so many holes that suspicion had to be focused on her. But did anyone else enter the frame as a suspect?

Patrick (Dutchy) Holland, a prime suspect in the murder of journalist Veronica Guerin, had a home in nearby Brittas Bay and was well known to the locals. He was regarded as one of Ireland's most dangerous and unpredictable criminals, and as a professional hit man. He knew the locality very well and was seen in Jack White's on many occasions. Locals described him as inoffensive, quiet, and a bit of a loner. He had spent his adult life in and out of prisons. (He died recently while serving a lengthy prison sentence for possessing drugs with intent to supply.) There was justification for regarding Holland as a likely suspect in the execution of Tom Nevin but not sufficient evidence to sustain a charge, or even to justify a charge being put against him.

Many criminals were named as likely suspects for the shooting, but evidence was never obtained to incriminate any of them.

Catherine had the most to gain from Tom Nevin's death: she would become sole owner of the pub, the properties in Dublin, and the proceeds of two substantial insurance policies on him.

Two unguarded and incriminating remarks by her contributed greatly to a suspicion that she was herself involved in the murder of her husband. First of all, on 19 March, in conversation with Detectives Joe Collins and Jim McCawl, she stated that 'the amount is in the books' – a reference to the day's takings. Neither Garda had any knowledge prior to this of any books, lodgements, or cash in the kitchen, where the body of her dead husband was lying. Tom had been doing the books when she went to bed, and she did not then, or indeed after the arrival of the Gardaí, enter the kitchen – if her account of events is to be believed. How then was she to know the amount that was in the cash books?

Secondly, she made reference to having got a smell of burning when she was in her bedroom. This was an attempt to convince everyone that she had been elsewhere when the fatal shot was fired; however, just a few minutes after the gunshot tests carried out by Gardaí, there was little if any smell remaining. Catherine's phenomenal sense of smell is just not credible, considering that it took her about an hour to free herself when she had been tied up in the bedroom.

Another factor was that the pub staff had been told by Catherine that they would not be staying at the pub on the night of 18/19 March – which was most unusual. Her own words were: 'No one, and I mean no one, is staying here tonight.' The staff from experience knew not to question a direct command from Catherine.

Other suspects had been speedily taken out of the frame, leaving one obvious remaining suspect: Catherine Nevin.

7

CATHERINE SCULLY AND TOM NEVIN

Catherine Nevin, née Scully, spent her formative years in Nurney, County Kildare. This is a small, close-knit community, which rarely hit the headlines before Catherine was to create unexpected interest in it.

Her parents were regarded as having been excellent neighbours, always willing to help those less fortunate than themselves. Patrick, her father, had a small farm, which provided life's essentials for his wife Mary and their three children, Catherine, Betty and Vincent. The latter, unfortunately, was stricken with polio at an early age, leaving him with a permanent limp.

Mary supplemented the family's meagre income by working as a seamstress. Their home has been unfairly described as a galvanised hovel. On the contrary, it was a very nice, well-kept house, small in size – as most Irish houses were when the Scully kids were growing up.

The children were happy and well cared for, similar to those in all the other families in the local community. All three were bright, particularly Catherine. She attended the local primary school in Nurney, and the Presentation College in Kildare town. She applied herself diligently to her studies, realising from an early age that a good education was essential for her future prospects.

Locals would describe Catherine as a pleasant, intelligent girl who was respectful to authority, and driven by a fierce determination to succeed in life. Nurney, and indeed the nearby towns, offered little in the way of meaningful employment, especially to an ambitious young girl such as Catherine, and she decided to seek fame and fortune in Dublin.

Dublin Castle Hotel, near O'Connell Street, a well-known republican haunt, required a receptionist. Opportunity beckoned, and Catherine seized it with open arms. It is debatable whether Catherine realised the reputation the hotel had acquired. If she did not, she would find out soon enough.

Catherine was at an impressionable age, and easily smitten with the idea of rubbing shoulders and conversing with such instantly recognisable personalities as Cathal Goulding, chief of staff of the Official IRA, and Joe Cahill, an active member of the Provisional IRA. She was frequently seen in conversation with them and would boast to her friends about her close friendship with them. It did not cause her any trepidation that these individuals, whom she admired so much, were regarded by most Irish citizens as being nothing more than low-life terrorists. Little time was wasted by her in lavishing attention on the likes of Goulding and Cahill.

Catherine was won over to Goulding and Cahill's intended political goals, and believed that her own ambitions could be realised more expeditiously with them as her confidantes and benefactors. She would not be the first to discover that she was embarking upon a very dangerous journey.

What attributes would Catherine rely on to achieve these ambitions? She regarded herself as intelligent, and despite any great academic achievements, she most certainly is. Attractive, yes, but nothing sensational. Perhaps what would advance her cause to a greater extent were characteristics which at that stage she may not even have realised she possessed, such as cunning, deviousness and criminal intent. These traits were being swiftly germinated.

The Sinn Féin Advice Centre in Finglas doubled as a TV repair/rental business. Catherine became a frequent visitor there and often sought the advice of one John Jones, who ran the centre. She would also later proposition him to kill her husband on at least six separate occasions.

Tom Nevin, born on 22 September 1941, was a native of Tynagh, County Galway. He was the eldest of six boys and three girls. The family had a medium-sized farm, sufficient to supply life's essentials. The work was hard. Farm machinery, such as tractors, milking parlours and the like, which are now an accepted part of every farmer's equipment, was a luxury in those days.

Tom, being the eldest son, would have inherited the farm had he chosen to do so. He had seen many of his friends turn their backs on the hardships of farming and head for Dublin or England. These departed friends by and large painted pictures of a five-day week, good pay, and plenty of social activity, so he decided to give this adventure a go.

Tom, at the tender age of seventeen, set off for the bright lights and the unknown world that was Dublin city. Having an uncle as licensee of Freehill's pub in Dolphins Barn was a bonus for the impressionable youth from Galway. He lived in his Uncle Willie's house and would later manage the pub owned by him. Lonely, and as yet without any new-found friends, he sought solace the only way he knew, and that was to get involved in the local GAA club – preferably one with a hurling tradition, his favourite sporting activity. Though not quite of inter-county standard, he was a better-than-average club hurler and would certainly have been welcomed with open arms by many Dublin clubs.

The country-boy tag was slowly but surely being replaced by one marked by maturity, ambition and contentment. Some of his friends would describe him as being frugal, others as being careful with his money. Tom, being easy on the eye to most girls, was not short of female company. He did not have any close or serious relationships until he met June O'Flanagan, a Mayo woman. They seemed to hit it off from the beginning. Both families were pleased with the match, and they married in April 1962. Their first residence was a rented flat on South Circular Road.

Tom had no intention of spending the rest of his life working as a barman, even as a bar manager, and had steely ambitions of one day owning his own pub. This, he felt, would not be achieved in his present employment. England beckoned, and though Tom and June remained there for a few years, and managed a pub, their life was not what they had expected. They returned to Ireland.

Tom got a job in the Inchicore area of Dublin, working in a pub. All was not as it should be in the marriage, and June would later take full responsibility for the breakdown of the relationship. Tom, she maintained, was a great, kind and loving man: 'a gentle giant'. The marriage was annulled.

Accounts about how and when Tom and Catherine first met differ. Catherine would give many versions. In court, she suggested that they had met in the Castle Hotel when she was employed there. An account given by her to the staff at Jack White's was that the happy occurrence had taken place at the Bachelor Festival in Lisdoonvarna, County Clare, in 1970, when she was nineteen.

As the romance blossomed, so too did Catherine's cunning, deviousness and evil intent. Tom had put his cards on the table about his first marriage to June O'Flanagan. Catherine's acceptance of Tom's previous marriage was reassuring, and perhaps even enhanced the high esteem in which she was now held by him. June may have been past history for Tom, but Catherine had questions she wanted answers to, and only June could provide them.

*

A careful plan had to be devised, and expertly executed, if Catherine was to gain the trust of June O'Flanagan for a meeting she was planning.

In June 1972, Catherine, resplendent as usual, knocked on the door of June's house in Clontarf, Dublin. She said she was a social worker and was greeted and admitted. No identification was requested or provided. Catherine, in her own inimitable way, put June at ease, and there was an instant rapport between them.

Catherine was meticulous in the choice of subjects she broached. It was imperative that she got to know more about Tom's first wife to find out if she was a person of substance, intelligence or beauty – and, most important of all, if she had any hold on Tom, either financially or otherwise. As Catherine's queries became somewhat more intense, June became apprehensive. Why, she wondered, had Tom given such detailed information about their marriage, their pending annulment, and their sex life to this woman? Still, the reassuring fact remained that this was a social worker doing an honest day's work.

Catherine got the answers she wanted: no, Tom had never strayed; no, a reunion was a total non-runner; and, most important of all, no, June would never make any financial claim on Tom, dead or alive. Satisfied at last that June would pose no problems in the future, the way was now clear for her to become Mrs Nevin.

8

THE BUSINESS OF MARRIAGE

Catherine had hoped for a spectacular wedding with all the trimmings, and of course the presence of personalities of note. Tom, who normally bowed to her wishes, on this occasion was adamant that a low-key affair, preferably in Rome, would be in better taste.

On 13 January 1976, the knot was tied in the church of St John Matimer, in Rome. Catherine was then twenty-five years of age, and many years Tom's junior. The innocent, impressionable girl had by now been replaced by a scheming, manipulative and aggressively ambitious woman.

After the wedding, Tom continued working at Freehill's pub, and Catherine, having completed a course in deportment and interview techniques at the University of Coleraine, travelled around the country lecturing to students. This was certainly more culturally acceptable to her than working in a pub. A modelling school was another venture Catherine had undertaken, with high hopes; but unfortunately for her, it turned out to be an unmitigated disaster financially. Tom's employment was not at all to her liking, however, and she began to seek out premises for sale or even lease. Her visits to the Sinn Féin Advice Centre became more frequent as her impatience with Tom's laid-back approach increased.

The couple moved to Mayfield Road, Dublin, to a substantial property containing seven flats. Visitors to their flat included Cathal Goulding, chief of staff of the IRA. It is reasonable to presume that his movements and contacts with associates were being monitored by the Special Branch. Catherine and Tom would also have come under scrutiny, and their affiliations, political and otherwise, would have been screened. Catherine's increasingly frequent visits to the Sinn Féin Advice Centre would also have increased Garda interest in them.

Catherine immersed herself in painting and decorating the flats at Mayfield Road. She also bought a house on South Circular Road. Next to be added to their property portfolio was a spacious house on Mountshannon Road, just off South Circular Road. Tom was definitely emerging as a person with an eye for a solid business transaction.

With the purchase of properties under their belts, and no great difficulties encountered, attention swung sharply towards the pub trade. Catherine's republican friends were courted continuously, in the hope that they would move Tom and herself towards an acceptable licensed premises. Such properties are not generally readily available and competition at that time was intense, especially in Dublin.

They steered her in the direction of the Barry House pub in Finglas, which, if secured by herself and Tom, would also be in Sinn Féin's interests. Not for nothing was it regarded as a well-known republican haunt. Though he had some reservations, Tom went along with the idea. It would at the very least be a stepping stone towards owning their own pub. The Barry House had been closed in 1984 because of continued assaults and malicious damage. It is located in a rough area where crime and criminal activity were part and parcel of everyday life. Because of its reputation for violence, there was no great interest in purchasing the lease. But with the assurances given by Sinn Féin, Tom and Catherine were not unduly worried about a continuance of such behaviour.

Immediately the Nevins took over the lease and moved into the premises, so too did the republicans. *An Phoblacht* newspaper was sold on the premises, and security was provided by the republican movement. The pub was of course being closely monitored by the Special Branch. Something akin to normality was restored at the pub, and any assaults or damage were swiftly and expertly dealt with by the bouncer provided by the IRA. However, Catherine's ambitions did not take long to resurface, as she tired of the surroundings and the unacceptable (to her) low-class clientele. Acceptable and affordable pubs in Dublin were just not within the couple's financial means. The only alternative was to look at suitable pubs outside the city.

9

THE PURCHASE OF JACK WHITE'S INN

Much waiting and frequent visits to pubs outside Dublin would eventually pay off. Both Tom and Catherine were won over by Jack White's Inn, which had been recommended to them by a republican confidante of Catherine's.

The pub is located on the main Dublin–Wexford road, six to seven miles north of Arklow town and forty-three miles south of Dublin. Business was mainly the pub trade and, to a lesser extent, a restaurant service. The building was impressive, though in need of refurbishment. Locals would form the nucleus of customers, and the ever-increasing population of Arklow town was also a positive for the business. In the hands of such a dynamic duo as Catherine and Tom, the possibilities were limitless.

Both were in unison: this was their dream, and a new start beckoned. The sale went through smoothly, and the price tag of £270,000 was no obstacle. The Barry House and its problems would soon be a thing of the past – but would Catherine's many sexual affairs? Though Tom was kept mainly in the dark about his wife's extra-marital affairs in Dublin, a key witness in the murder trial would state with conviction that Tom was well aware of her exploits.

One of the willing helpers during the move was none other than William (Willie) McClean, Catherine's lover. He claimed that Tom definitely knew of this liaison. McClean, whose evidence was later to be a key part of the State's case against Catherine, first met her in a pub in Dublin. He admitted that he was somewhat smitten by Catherine, and her obvious interest in him.

She presented herself to him as a woman of considerable means; this was clearly the case, as shown by her attire, and her expensive jewellery. Quite out of the blue, she suggested a sexual encounter, and they began a torrid, passionate, and potentially dangerous affair that would last eighteen months. At the outset, Willie was somewhat puzzled by her attention. He saw what he regarded as an attractive, well-heeled woman seeking comforts of the flesh with an out-of-work, married man who had little to offer materially. He would not seek answers, but would play her for what he could. This was an art he had perfected over the years.

This was not Catherine's first affair and most definitely would not be her last. Willie left her under no illusions about himself and his past – which he readily admits he is not proud of. (Among other things, he fathered children outside his marriage.) Friends who knew him in his twenties and thirties described him as not bad-looking, slim with blonde hair. However, by the time he and Catherine met, he had degenerated into a grossly overweight, red-faced, bulbous-nosed man. He retained his rough charm, wit, and ability to seduce women such as Catherine.

Tom and Catherine moved into Jack White's Inn on 2 May 1986. Locals, sensing a new and hopefully exciting new era for the pub, were eagerly awaiting developments. Little if anything was known of Tom and Catherine except perhaps by the local Gardaí, who, as a matter of course, would have obtained background information on all new owners taking over licensed premises in their area.

It was not long before Catherine wanted the pub to have a

'better' clientele. Yes, she was at last joint owner of a pub with her husband, but it was, and would remain, an ordinary country pub, unless immediate remedial action was taken. A hairdressing salon was quickly put in place, the building was redecorated, and the food menu was improved. Word quickly spread, and Jack White's Inn soon became known for its excellent restaurant. Catherine was gaining a reputation as a fine chef. Trade picked up: they were off to a good start. But Catherine still wanted to see celebrities and dignitaries in the pub.

10

FRIENDSHIPS

Gardaí would have a part to play in her plans. With them on her side, many benefits would follow – or so she thought. Catherine was aware of a tradition in rural Ireland whereby Gardaí would be offered an occasional free drink, whether they were on or off duty, by pub owners. She would offer and, if the offer was accepted, it would become a regular occurrence – and could place the Garda in a compromising position.

Even in those early days of their stewardship, stories were circulating about late-night revelling and after-hours drinking involving Gardaí – though complaints were never made to the relevant authorities. The first-known Garda member holding high office to become a frequent visitor at the pub was Inspector Tom Kennedy. Most of his duties were filling in for superintendents who were absent for various reasons in Wexford, Gorey, Enniscorthy, New Ross and Wicklow. He lived in Wicklow town and would pass the pub frequently. A middle-aged, married man with a grown-up family, he was well liked by colleagues and the public alike. It was not long before Catherine was providing him with free drinks and meals. His presence at the pub was an irritant to some of the local

Gardaí, who viewed him as an intrusion, mainly because of his rank.

Catherine's familiarity with customers did not extend to women – for obvious reasons. Catherine, especially with drink on board, was an insensitive and outrageous flirt. She showed scant regard for the feelings of wives or girlfriends, and as a result she was despised by them. It didn't take long before male customers heavily outnumbered females at Jack White's – much to Catherine's delight.

The selection of staff, which consisted mostly of young schoolgirls, would be the sole preserve of Catherine. She was the queen bee, and as such would not be outshone by any young upstarts. Dress came in for special attention: skirts were to be of sufficient length to cover the knees, and blouses were under no circumstances to display any cleavage. Friendliness with customers was essential, but even the slightest hint of flirting would result in a stiff reprimand, or even dismissal. Duties were carefully and meticulously explained, and none of the girls were left under any illusions as to the high standards demanded by Catherine.

Dress discipline expected from the staff did not extend to the boss. Her daily appearances were the subject of much comment and even suppressed giggles. Her mostly seductive clothing was complemented by daily hairdos, heavy makeup and manicures; she was described by staff members as mutton dressed as lamb. Despite this, she was not without her admirers.

Arrangements were being put in place for the official opening. Invitations were dispatched to locals, republican friends, politicians and people Catherine regarded as key personalities, locally and nationally. Unfortunately for Catherine, there was no influx of her chosen personalities at the opening. Known criminals from Dublin were in attendance, as was Cathal Goulding, the chief of staff of the IRA. Some members of the Sinn Féin Advice Centre attended; others chose to give the event the cold shoulder. Some of her lovers past and present were also there.

In 1985, Jack White's Inn had been broken into, and the then owners, Peter Doyle and his family, were robbed at gunpoint. After a lengthy investigation, headed by myself, two well-known criminals from Dublin, Michael Cribben and Paul Harte, were arrested, charged and convicted. On the return journey from that trial, I briefly stopped at Jack White's, now under the control of its new owners, the Nevins, though I did not know them then. As I drank a pint of Guinness, a young waitress approached and told me that Mrs Nevin requested me to avail of the facilities in 'the special room'. I thanked the young girl and declined. Mention should perhaps be made that I had by then been promoted to the rank of inspector and was stationed in Bray, County Wicklow. I considered this offer to be most unusual, but better was to follow.

I was still living in Gorey, and passed Jack White's on average three times a week while I was going to and coming from work. One evening, an off-duty Garda from Arklow asked me to join him for a drink. I agreed, and we also ordered a meal. When I called a waitress over so that we could pay the bill, the garda casually informed me: 'There's no need for that here. You don't pay here.' My terse reply – 'You may not, but I do' – seemed to take him by surprise. After this encounter, my suspicions as to rumours circulating about the premises, the owners and the Gardaí intensified.

In September 1989, I was promoted to superintendent and was allocated Gorey Garda District, which encompasses Gorey, Arklow, Bunclody, Carnew and Courtown. I was also selected to attend a course at Hiltrup Police Academy, Münster, West Germany. Inspector Tom Kennedy took charge of Gorey Garda District in my absence.

I returned to Ireland in December 1989 – to tales of unusual happenings in my office during my absence. The district clerk (my secretary and right-hand man), a man of strict principles, seemed ill at ease with the inspector's behaviour. A blonde woman driving a big car had been a regular caller, and on each occasion she had asked to see Inspector Kennedy. She would be brought to his temporary office. These visits were eventually to take a bizarre twist. The clerk, unaware that the inspector had company, entered the office and found the blonde sitting on Tom's knees behind the desk, in a position best described as comfortable. There were no bodies falling or jumping from the chair at this unexpected intrusion. They did as on all other occasions when she called: he locked the office, and both of them left together in her car. It didn't take long to discover that the blonde was none other than Catherine Nevin. The penny was beginning to drop. It appeared to him that the two were involved in something other than having a chat.

My next encounter with Catherine was while I was returning from a Leinster hurling game in Croke Park one day with three friends, and we decided to stop off at Jack White's for a meal and drinks. A few minutes after our entrance, a young waitress approached me to say: 'Superintendent, Mrs Nevin has instructed that your party should be shown to "the special room" for your meal.' As the pub was packed, mostly with Wexford supporters, this offer was gladly accepted.

Steaks for all and a bottle of wine was the order. When the meals arrived, there were two steaks on each plate and a bottle of red wine, in addition to the white wine which we had ordered. Desserts arrived as ordered – but so too did Irish coffees, which we had not ordered.

I requested the bill, only to be politely told by the young waitress: 'Mrs Nevin has ordered me not to accept any payment, as this is her treat.' I insisted on paying and asked to see Mr or Mrs Nevin, only to be told: 'They are too busy, and Mrs Nevin is adamant I am not under any circumstances to accept payment.'

My friends appreciated the embarrassing position I had been placed in. A solution was quickly arrived at: the cost of what we had eaten and drunk was calculated, and we decided to purchase a framed painting costing that amount. One of my friends later left the painting into the pub with a note thanking the owners for the facilities they had provided.

Though having caught a fleeting glimpse of Catherine, I had not actually been introduced to her. To satisfy my curiosity, I called to the pub around June 1992. A friend of mine, since deceased, was chatting to a blonde lady at the bar – of course, none other than Catherine Nevin. He introduced us, and the conversation flowed. My friend, being involved in the wholesale food industry, had Catherine as one of his customers. It was inevitable that food should figure prominently in the conversation, and she asked me what my favourite seafood was. Oysters, I replied.

Conversation was switched deliberately by Catherine to her friends and acquaintances. She boasted about having met Assistant Garda Commissioner Pat Byrne (later to become garda commissioner) and Chief Superintendent Pat Crummy, the officer then in charge of Wexford Division. Tom Kennedy was the last of this important triumvirate. Interestingly, I was the missing cog, being the superintendent with responsibility for Gorey Garda District, which included Ballynapark, the townland in which Jack White's Inn is located.

Her list of properties in Dublin was also made known to me. Though I placed no significance on it then, she alleged to have a share in a TV shop in Finglas. This TV shop (which was also a Sinn Féin advice centre), would later be of huge significance in the murder investigation. Her desire to impress was so obvious, and her list of financial achievements so uninteresting, that it was a relief for me to leave. I saw her as a foul-mouthed, suggestive and disgusting woman. Her actions when seated on the bar stool were totally provocative. She kept crossing her legs and revealing as much leg as the slit in her skirt would allow. It was so disgusting as to be also slightly amusing.

This was my first meeting with Catherine Nevin, about whom I had heard so much, most of it from members of the Gardaí. By and large, many were singing her praises to me. One was loud in his praise of her generosity, as he and his wife had dined at Jack White's, and she wouldn't under any circumstances accept payment for the meal. The same individual wouldn't have twisted her arm to make sure she accepted payment of the bill, however. All in all, during those early days Catherine was very much the flavour of the month.

God loves a trier, and some days later my trust in that adage took on an added significance. A neatly packed parcel addressed to me was delivered to my office. It contained one dozen oysters and a simple note which read: 'Pat, enjoy these, Catherine.' I called to one of the local supermarkets, where (fortunately) oysters were on sale. Noting the price, I sent a cheque for the appropriate amount to Catherine.

I later received a note, which read 'Pat, this was not meant as a sale, but a gift, Catherine'. Attached to the note was my cheque; I had Detectives Jim McCawl and Joe Collins initial and date the cheque, and I filed it away for future reference, if necessary. Any other contacts I had thereafter with Catherine Nevin were confined to business-related matters, such as licensing applications.

On one occasion, she made an application under the licensing laws, which necessitated a viewing of the facilities available at the pub. Detective Jim McCawl accompanied me to the pub. Catherine insisted that we have two of her coffee specials; after supplying them, she absented herself briefly. Jim took a sip from the cup, then swiftly and neatly tipped the remaining contents into a nearby plant container. 'She's fucking laced it with whiskey,' said Jim. I agreed with him as I polished off the special. Catherine was unaware that Jim was a nondrinker. Seeing Jim's cup empty, and expressing delight that the drink had been so speedily dispatched by him, she quickly supplied a refill. This received a similar fate to its predecessor. I found the incident hilarious; Jim didn't.

As time moved on, my distrust and apprehension about Catherine grew. This culminated in my taking a stance whereby under no circumstances would I have any dealings with her without another member of An Garda Síochána being present.

11

GARDAÍ WHELAN AND MURPHY

On 13 July 1992, Chief Superintendent Pat Crummy, Wexford, requested my presence at his office as a matter of urgency. He informed me that Catherine Nevin had made a written complaint about Gardaí Vincent Whelan and Michael Murphy. The complaints were of a criminal nature; if proven, they could have dire consequences, including dismissal, for both officers.

There was something strange and unusual about what I had been told. Unusual, because her complaint had been made to, and taken by, a chief superintendent. Normal procedure is that a person with a complaint against a Garda goes to the Garda Complaints Board, or alternatively the local garda station. A meeting may be sought with a higher rank and would be granted, if possible. Rarely, if ever, does a chief superintendent deal with such issues (though of course he or she is fully justified in doing so).

Shortly after my meeting with Crummy, a surprise visitor to my office was Detective Superintendent Tom Connolly, Investigation Section, Garda Headquarters. He had not known me previously. He had, he informed me, been appointed to investigate the complaints. He outlined the complaints and asked my opinion, which was: 'I don't believe a fucking word of it.'

He knew nothing of Gardaí Murphy and Whelan before being appointed to investigate the complaints against them. One must also presume that he knew nothing of Catherine Nevin. Gardaí Murphy and Whelan, and their families, were facing years of unjustified and cruel punishment on the mainly unsupported word of a woman who would later become known nationally, even internationally, as a cruel, vicious murderess.

The complaints made by Catherine against Garda Murphy were of indecent assault on Catherine and on a teenage female employee, as well as corruption, and of corruption against Whelan. The corruption allegation is significant, as its falsity is so evident. On 16 January 1989, Catherine applied at Arklow District Court for a restaurant certificate. Normal and required procedure was adhered to, and the notice of intent was sent to the superintendent's office in Gorey. Inspector Tom Kennedy was filling in for the superintendent, who had in fact retired and had not at that time been replaced; Inspector Kennedy informed the court that there was no Garda objection to this. He would be merely informing the court of the attitude of Arklow Gardaí to the application.

Catherine alleged that Murphy had demanded £1,000 to ensure the success of the application. But she was a good friend of Inspector Kennedy, who alone could object to the application in court on behalf of the Gardaí. Murphy would have no input whatever to the application.

To add insult to injury, her second complaint was a repeat of the first on the certificate being renewed on 2 October 1989. She allegedly paid Murphy another £1,000, again demanded by him. Judge Sean McGee granted the renewal and Inspector Kennedy once more represented the Gardaí.

If Catherine is to be believed, Murphy was still not satisfied, and his unquenchable thirst for dirty money continued unabated. The renewal date this time around was September 1990; again, the usual fee of £1,000 was sought, but on this occasion it was refused by Catherine, as Kennedy advised her not to pay. On hearing her refusal to pay up, Murphy allegedly told her to 'Fuck off'. The certificate was renewed without any garda objection.

Murphy's appetite for cash didn't stop there, she would have everyone believe. He asked for £1,000 to give assistance in an assault case brought by a previous employee, Larry Darcy, against Tom. Murphy was to influence Darcy not to make a complaint. Rather stupidly, one must surmise, she paid up, even though this did not prevent Darcy from pursuing – and winning on appeal – an action against the Nevins.

In her statement to Chief Superintendent Crummy on 13 July 1992, Catherine stated: 'I know what happened was irregular, but in this business backhanders are common enough. But I felt at the time, and still do, that this was a way of getting the certificate when everything was just not right.' Her conduct makes her guilty of bribery and corruption, but no investigation into this was ever carried out. One has to wonder why.

Another of her statements deals with the allegation of indecent assault by Garda Murphy. She alleged that on the night of 26 August 1991, after midnight, 'Garda Murphy came up behind me in the bar when I was getting a whiskey for him and pinned me to the ice-maker. I was aware he had himself exposed. He pulled my skirt up and tried to force himself into me.' (Garda Murphy at all times denied this allegation, and when the relevant investigation file was sent to the DPP, he directed that there should be no criminal proceeding against him.)

Where was Tom and the staff when this brazen and serious indecent assault was taking place? Tom was in fact just a few feet away in the kitchen doing the books, as was his routine at the close of the day's business. The staff would have been cleaning up or having a drink.

Perhaps the most devious complaint of Catherine's concerned an alleged indecent assault by Murphy on a seventeen-year-old female employee. On 13 July 1992, Chief Superintendent Crummy interviewed the girl at Jack White's licensed premises. She dated the alleged indecent assault by Garda Murphy on her as having taken place on or about 8 August 1990. Catherine, in her statement on 18 July, claimed that the assault took place on 20 July 1990. Both statements were taken two years after the alleged incident. Why the delay in reporting such a serious incident involving a local Garda? The girl's account was brief, informative and to the point. Additional damning statements were made by the girl against other Gardaí who, she said, would frequent the pub when on night duty. They would be supplied with food and drink free of charge.

She was to sensationally deny the truthfulness of her statements when she went to Arklow Bay Hotel with Paddy Doyle and his wife (near neighbours, and customers at the pub) on 22 August 1992. Doyle, in a written statement, said she told him: 'If I tell you the truth will you promise not to tell anyone, because if Catherine found out she would kill me. I never had anything to do with Murphy. Catherine told the Dublin Gardaí that Murphy forced me to have oral sex with him about two and a half to three years ago. I had to make a statement about it, because I could not let Catherine down. She told me if I stood by her, she would pay for me to go back to college for two years, or I could have a full-time job in the bar at Jack White's.'

On 5 September 1992, the Doyles met Catherine and the girl at The Tap, a local pub. Catherine was very drunk, and informed Paddy that she had been in Dublin giving statements about 'the other bastard, Murphy . . . for what he has done to that young girl, he will never wear a uniform again. If only the locals knew the sums of money I had paid to him for not summonsing locals leaving Jack White's with beer on them. I knew about the Protestants he tried to get money from for different things. Murphy will go down for life for what he did to the girl.'

The following day, Tom Nevin and the girl called to Doyle's house. She had been drunk the previous night, was upset about phone calls being received by her mother, and wondered if either of the Doyles was responsible. Paddy pointed out that he did not know her surname, or her mother's phone number. He then asked the girl, in the presence of Tom: 'Did anything happen between you and Murphy?' She replied: 'No, but I have to back Catherine.'

Doyle also said that, on 7 September 1992, Inspector Kennedy confronted him in the car park at Jack White's, saying: 'The very man I want to see. You were doing a lot of talking over the weekend. If the big boys from Dublin find out, you're in trouble.'

The only complaint involving Garda Whelan relates to Catherine's allegation that after paying Murphy £1,000 for the restaurant certificates, she saw him handing some of it to Whelan in the patrol car outside the pub.

Catherine's story was evidently accepted by the hierarchy at Garda Headquarters. They ordered the suspension of the two Gardaí, who were subsequently arrested, detained and placed in cells. They were both later cleared of any wrongdoing.

There was no obvious answer as to why there was such a sudden and instant turnaround in her attitude towards the local Gardaí. She would continue to defame them individually and collectively to locals, who by and large regarded her rantings as those of a woman scorned.

The local Gardaí started to give the pub a wide berth. They were determined that what Catherine had foisted upon their colleagues would not happen to them. They could not stop her from making further spurious complaints against Arklow-based Gardaí, but they could – and did – stop frequenting the pub.

12

PREVIOUS EXPLOITS

As the early stages of the investigation progressed, there was still no suspect other than Catherine being seriously considered. Names, mostly well-known Dublin criminals with a reputation for gun violence, were mentioned, but they were kept on the back burner until something substantive against them could be unearthed. Instead, a trawl into some of Catherine's shady deals began.

The assault case brought by Larry Darcy against Tom Nevin is one example. Darcy claimed that he was severely assaulted by Tom at the pub on 23 December 1988, while Catherine was present. However, he declined to make a written statement or to pursue a criminal investigation. Civil proceedings were later taken by him. Judge Sean Magee, after hearing the evidence, found in favour of Tom Nevin. At the hearing, Anthony Doyle, Redcross, County Wicklow, stated that it was he and not Tom who had assaulted Darcy. Darcy appealed the decision and Judge Smith rejected the evidence of Doyle in its entirety. He awarded Darcy £2,500 damages plus costs.

On 5 February 1993, a near neighbour of Anthony Doyle's reported to Gardaí that Doyle had received £300 from the Nevins to give false evidence that he had assaulted Darcy. Anthony Doyle was interviewed and made a written statement in which he outlined having been approached by Catherine Nevin and offered money to say in court that he had assaulted Larry Darcy. He gave the false evidence, as prepared and dictated to him.

Detective Jim McCawl interviewed Catherine about the allegations. She informed him: 'I have not discussed that case with anyone, other than my husband and solicitor.' She then got a sheet of paper and wrote the name and address of her solicitor on it and gave it to McCawl. Scowling, she told him: 'I had no conversation with Anthony Doyle about my husband's case. See my lips, there was no conversation with him.' A file was prepared and submitted, but the case did not proceed.

In September of that year, Catherine made allegations concerning McCawl and Anthony Doyle. She regarded McCawl's conduct as aggressive and unacceptable. The complaint was investigated and McCawl was fully exonerated.

At about 8 PM on 20 November 1991, Catherine Nevin walked into Pearse Street Garda Station in Dublin. She claimed that, as she was driving through Dolphins Barn, a youth jumped in front of her car, forcing her to stop. A second youth smashed the front passenger window and grabbed two packages from the floor of the car. These packages contained the cash lodgement from the pub (£4,500), plus additional cash, which brought the total to £5,786. She said that she had intended lodging the money in the bank, but was late. Of interest is the fact she was collected at the garda station by Inspector Tom Kennedy.

In the search at Jack White's after Tom's murder, a cash book was seized, in which the week 10 to 16 November 1991 was included. A lodgement slip dated 18 November 1991 shows the pub lodgement as £3,675.26, flats (rental income from properties) £300 and hair salon £108; total amount £4,083.26. A bank statement issued by Allied Irish Bank shows that a lodgement of £4,083.26 was made to the Nevins' account on 18 November.

This indicates that she did not have the money in her car on 20 November. The insurance company settled the subsequent claim for £1,500: breaches of the conditions of the policy were cited as the reason for nonpayment of the outstanding amount.

Inspector Kennedy alleged that Tom and Catherine Nevin told him on 5 December 1993 that jewellery, including her wedding ring, was stolen from her bedroom. Catherine made a claim and received a settlement of £1,685.

Was Kennedy, as a knowledgeable member of An Garda Síochána, unaware that all such reports are to be recorded in official Garda records? Yet Kennedy didn't do so, either due to a lapse of memory or perhaps because he didn't think it necessary or relevant.

Kennedy's version of the reappearance of the most valuable heirloom, both intrinsically and sentimentally – the wedding ring – was listened to with interest. Tom Kennedy, in an interview with the Gardaí, said that on 4 April 1996, Catherine showed him her wedding ring, saying: 'That ring was stolen and Tom recovered it for me. He arrived home from Dublin with it on a Monday night, about the middle of February 1996, after many months of painstaking efforts to recover it.' Kennedy felt that this might have significance to the murder investigation, as it had been taken from Catherine's bedroom.

Catherine suggested during Garda interviews that her husband must have recovered it from his criminal contacts in Dublin, or maybe even from a pawnbrokers, mentioning one in particular, Brereton's. Tom was apparently determined to recover his wife's stolen ring. On many occasions after returning late from his regular trips to Dublin, he would attribute his lateness to efforts at finding the ring. She said she was taken aback when Tom handed her the stolen wedding ring on 12 February 1996, saying: 'That is the one I gave you twenty years ago, wear it now. I said I would get it back for you and I did.' Tom Kennedy said to Detective Sergeant O'Brien: 'It's extraordinary the bold Tom recovered it. It's an extraordinary story after that length of time.'

Extraordinary yes, if one was gullible enough to believe it. Enquiries were made at all pawnbrokers, with negative results, and similarly at all auction rooms. Tom Nevin never visited or made enquiries from them about the missing wedding ring. Catherine was concerned that some of the investigation team may have seen the ring, and rather than face difficult questioning on the subject, decided to report that it had been recovered. She was also of course trying to portray an image of an idyllic marriage, when in fact it had long since fallen apart.

The number of claims Catherine pursued against insurance companies was nothing short of startling. In all, there were in excess of ten, mostly consisting of claims for larcenies, storm or flood damage, and fire damage. Settlements were made in most of the cases, and these settlements ranged from £124 to £2,000.

There were also claims of burglaries: in all, twelve were reported as having taken place at Jack White's pub between 1986 and January 1995. Of significance is one committed on 17 December 1988, involving the larceny of cash from the premises. Anthony Doyle was one of the two charged and convicted of this crime. Despite this, Catherine had the gall to approach him to give false evidence for her husband – which he agreed to do.

All available information had been gathered on Tom and Catherine Nevin but nothing of a serious nature was unearthed about Tom. It was unanimously accepted by the investigation team that he had played no more than a passive role, if any, in Catherine's corrupt past. He was a quiet, inoffensive man who was apparently afraid of his wife and what she was capable of doing.

The act of pulling the trigger that discharged the fatal shot against her husband could not perhaps be attributed to Catherine, but the detectives were satisfied beyond all reasonable doubt that she had had some involvement in the crime. However, as the investigation progressed, their suspicions were not substantiated by any hard evidence.

The lifestyle enjoyed by Catherine pre-19 March 1996 was resumed shortly after the funeral services. There was a time for mourning, and these obligations, she felt, had been fully and passionately fulfilled. Now there was a business to be run, properties in Dublin to be looked after, and many new opportunities and challenges to be faced – not least whether she could cope with the mounting garda suspicion centred on her.

13

THE SEARCH OF THE PUB

On 12 April 1996, Detective Sergeant Fergus O'Brien and Detective Joe Collins had a discussion with Catherine in her sitting room. These visits were openly accepted and did not seem to cause her unease. She had intimated previously that they were the only two Gardaí she had confidence in.

During the course of the conversation, Catherine left the room, leaving her diary lying open on a table. The opened page contained a phone number and beside it the name 'Heapes'. The detectives both took down the number and name to have them checked. The name 'Heapes' was known to Fergus O'Brien, though in what context he wasn't sure at that stage.

On 18 May 1996, the pub and residence was thoroughly and meticulously searched. Catherine was present throughout and didn't raise any objections. Assorted papers and documents were seized, including the diary. O'Brien and Collins noted the entries that they had seen in it on 12 April were now scribbled out.

Also found in the search were two pieces of paper, one with a phone number and the other a car number. The phone number, found in Catherine's bedroom, was evidently a Dublin number with a missing digit. It suggested that the number had been written prior to April 1994, when Dublin phone numbers increased to seven digits. Enquiries at Telecom Éireann indicated that the number was allocated to John Jones, and the missing digit was supplied.

John Jones was born on 12 November 1944 and was married with two children. During the years 1984 to 1988, he and Dessie Ellis ran the TV sales and repair shop, trading as Channel Vision, which doubled as the Sinn Féin advice centre which had previously been frequented by Catherine.

Jones had fallen foul of the law on one occasion in 1988, when he was given a three-year suspended sentence for receiving a stolen car. He was also ordered to pay £3,000 to the insurance company and £500 to the rightful owner of the car.

The phone number written in Catherine's diary was traced to William Adams, who had at one time employed Gerry Heapes. Heapes could best be described as someone with an interesting past. Born on 28 May 1950 in Dublin, and married with five children, his previous employments included work as a porter at Jervis Street Hospital and as a bouncer at various nightclubs in Dublin. He was involved with Sinn Féin/the Provisional IRA in the 1970s.

On 26 November 1977, he was caught red-handed by the Gardaí with eight others in an armed robbery at Leydon's Cash & Carry in Fairview, Dublin. At the Special Criminal Court, he was convicted of armed robbery and sentenced to ten years' imprisonment. He was released in April 1985 and became a frequent visitor at the Sinn Féin advice centre. It was there that he first met Catherine Nevin; he was later invited to the official opening of Jack White's Inn.

The car registration number led to William McClean, mentioned earlier as Catherine's lover. He has convictions recorded against him in the Republic and also Northern Ireland. On 26 July 1973 at Clogher Magistrates Court, he was found guilty of theft by deception and sentenced to three months in prison. On 2 October 1973, at Portadown Court, he was convicted of criminal deception and sentenced to two years' imprisonment, and on 15 April 1988 he was bound by Dublin District Court to keep the peace for six months for false pretences.

Catherine had dangerously sought the confidence and silence of not one but three individuals, all of whom had previous criminal convictions. It was perhaps because of the seedy pasts of Jones, Heapes and McClean that Catherine set out to gain their support for plans she had been devising over a number of years. They were not to suspect the evil propositions she would one day put to them individually.

14

THE STAFF AND PATRONS

The staff at Jack White's Inn were to supply information that would prove to be of great assistance to the investigation. They were mostly young girls, many of whom had only temporary employment. Some of the girls, fearful about Catherine's legendary temper, were somewhat apprehensive about supplying written statements. However, none of them refused to supply a statement. Catherine would be portrayed as a woman with a fearful temper, and a dangerous lust for the opposite sex.

As the pub business got back to near-normality, Catherine's mind was already in overdrive, and she was being unusually kind and helpful to the girls. She was going out of her way to get them on her side, aware that they would soon be interviewed by the Gardaí about events leading up to, and after, the murder. There is no doubt that she was fearful of what damaging disclosures the staff might make about her. They had suffered untold mental stress because of the treatment meted out to them by Catherine, who seemed to delight in humiliating them, especially if any of her so-called celebrities were within earshot. The younger girls in particular were singled out by her. Now they had stories to tell, the contents of which could, and would, seriously trouble Catherine.

They had seen her treatment and hatred of Tom Nevin, her boasts that they were no longer married, her extra-marital affairs, her utterances that the pub would be sold, her dangerous temper, and her solicitations of Anthony Doyle to perjure himself. She asked the staff daily: 'Were the Guards talking to you?' 'What questions did they ask about me?' 'Did you make a statement?' 'What was in it?'

Eileen Byrne worked in Jack White's in 1993 as a cleaner for about six months. She left because of the unkind way Catherine treated the staff. She said tension was always evident between Tom and Cathcrine. The night after Tom Kennedy's retirement party, Byrne started work at 8 AM and saw four or five Gardaí drinking at the bar with Catherine. Tom was behind the bar and was agitated. He said to Eileen: 'This will end in tears.' When she was cleaning the men's toilet, she heard a noise behind her. She asked if someone was there. Judge O'Buachalla appeared, and she asked him: 'Could you not have told me you were there?' He replied: 'It's a free country.' If the judge came in for breakfast, Catherine was to be informed, and she would join him. He would phone occasionally and say that he was on his way. Referring to Gardaí Murphy and Whelan, Catherine had said: 'They'll never do their duty again. They'll never go out on the streets again.'

Elaine McDonagh outlined how Catherine had thrown a knife at her in the kitchen, but fortunately it had missed her. Catherine was angry about the fact that the plate-warmer hadn't been turned on and the food was being served on cold plates.

Brendan McGraynor recalled receiving a request over the phone from a lady about two or three weeks before St Patrick's weekend in 1996, seeking bed and breakfast for that holiday weekend. Catherine instructed him to refuse the booking as they were booked out. This was untrue: no bookings had been taken.

Cecelia McDonald worked as a cook at the pub for five years, from 1991 to 1996. She was always paid in cash but on St Patrick's weekend 1996, Catherine paid her by cheque.

Caroline Strahan made a very interesting statement. She started work at the pub in September 1991, and stayed two years. She said: 'In the summer of 1992, two Guards from Wicklow came looking for Superintendent Tom Kennedy. I knew he was up with Catherine and went up to tell her. When I knocked and opened the door I saw Tom Kennedy in the bed with her; they were under the covers and Tom had nothing on top. Catherine started panicking, came down after me and went in behind the bar.'

Strahan made another written statement in which she states: 'Tom and Catherine Nevin never got on; they were sleeping in separate bedrooms. I saw them, Kennedy and Catherine, in her bed loads of times. Catherine used to ring down and I'd bring breakfast up to them. They didn't care that I'd seen them. Tom Nevin knew this was going on but he never said anything.'

Adrienne Fisher made a statement on 19 April 1996. She worked at the pub for two and a half years, during which she remembers the judge calling regularly to the pub. She recalls Catherine saying: 'The judge is lovely.' She felt that Tom Nevin was for some unknown reason afraid of Catherine, as when they had one of their many arguments he was always the one to back down. Catherine also boasted about a boyfriend she had in Northern Ireland. Fisher highlights Catherine's republican tendencies and loathing for English people, which she once displayed on seeing English customers in the bar, who were complaining about the food. Catherine said: 'Are those fucking English bastards coming over here complaining? Do they think they own the fucking place?'

Fiona Lawlor was surprised that Catherine paid her by cheque the holiday weekend of Tom's murder. She thought this was unusual, as it was the first time during her employment at the pub that she had been paid her wages by cheque.

Catherine McGraynor worked as a waitress/chef part time at the pub for two years, in 1995 and 1996. In her statement, she recalls that at around midnight on 18 March, a taxi arrived to take the staff to a disco in Arklow. Catherine informed them that no one was staying overnight at the pub. This was the first time that Catherine had ever issued such a command to them.

Bernie Fleming worked at the pub full time from 8 March 1995. In her statement, she said she had a key to the front door, and the only other key holders were Tom, Catherine and Liz Hudson. There was a spare set hanging on a rack on the left side of the front hallway. Some six or seven weeks before the murder, Tom Nevin asked if she had seen them, as they were missing. She then asked Catherine about them and was told 'Donnacha O'Buachalla has them' but not to tell Tom. Within the next day or two, the keys appeared back on the rack in the hallway. O'Buachalla was later to deny under oath in the Central Criminal Court that he ever had these or any other keys for the premises.

During the month prior to the murder, a male caller giving the name John Ferguson phoned on several occasions. Catherine had warned Fleming that no matter where she was or what she was doing, when this man phoned Fleming was to get her immediately. His identity was unknown at that stage, and Catherine was later to deny repeatedly that she had any knowledge of a John Ferguson, or that she had received phone calls from a person using that name.

On 18 March 1996, Fleming was working as usual. That night, Catherine was sitting at the bar with a glass in front of her. She seemed uneasy, and not her usual self. At 11 PM, Catherine announced that she was going to check on the washing machine, which is in a little room on the ground floor just off the hairdressing salon. There is a door from this room out into the car park. Fleming was surprised at Catherine's newfound interest in the washing machine. She had never previously shown any interest in the washing machine, or the room in which it was kept; in fact, she didn't even know how to use the machine. When Catherine returned some minutes later, Fleming and Liz Hudson went to the washing machine to put on another load, but were amazed to discover that the washing machine was empty and had not been used. Catherine had told them that the wash she had put on had fifteen minutes to go.

Another unexplained happening was also noted by Bernie. That night she glanced into the restaurant and saw that the curtains were pulled – the first time she had ever seen them pulled. In fact, they are for effect only, and are not meant to be pulled.

She also said that early in the day, she saw that Catherine was wearing the normal amount of jewellery: her wedding ring, a watch and maybe a necklace. Later that night, Fleming noticed that she was wearing an excessive amount of jewellery: rings on all fingers, four or five chains on her neck, and a thick gold bracelet with emerald stones set in it.

Finishing her statement, she states: 'Tom was well aware Catherine was having affairs with a number of men. She did this openly and they would sleep in her room.' She said she had seen Tom Kennedy in Catherine's bedroom.

Ciara Tallon worked at the pub as a waitress during the summer of 1995. She got off to a bad start with Catherine, who reprimanded her for the dress she was wearing: it was too short. She remembers the judge calling to the pub. They were under strict orders from Catherine as to how to behave in his presence. He had his own menu, and his own seat in the conservatory.

Anne Marie Finnerty, a niece of Tom Nevin's, called to the pub in August 1995. During a conversation, Catherine informed her: 'We're thinking of selling the pub, in fact it will probably be sold before Christmas.' Tom and herself were, she stated, separating.

Una Doogue worked at the pub from March until September 1994, and again during the summer of the following year. She got to know O'Buachalla and Kennedy, who were frequent visitors. One day Catherine stated: 'There are two ways Tom Nevin would kill himself: it would be either in the car with drink taken, or during the course of a break-in because he would have drink in him.' Quite a prophetic statement, and one no doubt Catherine thought the Gardaí would be gullible enough to swallow.

Jane Murphy, a small, frail woman, worked as a cleaner for ten years at the pub. Of all the staff, Jane, or 'Jeanie', as she was commonly known, was the one who could best give an accurate account of Catherine and Tom and the happenings at the pub over the years.

About four years before the murder, she recalls Catherine and Tom having a flaming row. 'They were going to Spain on holidays, and their passports couldn't be found. But in truth, they could have by Tom, who had hid them because he didn't want to go on holidays with Catherine.' Jeanie knew where the passports were, got them, and handed them to the feuding couple. Tom wasn't amused.

Tom's dislike for Judge O'Buachalla was also well known to Jeanie. A few weeks before the murder, Tom told her that if the judge rang, she was to get him. True to form, he did phone, and Jeanie, being the good and loyal servant, got Tom. His choice of words and apparent anger towards the judge took her by surprise. 'I heard Tom fucking and blinding the judge, telling him to fuck off.'

According to Jeanie, Catherine gave Jessica Hunter 'a fierce time' for telling the Gardaí about her various partners. She didn't sack her because Jessica 'will give them more fucking information'. Jessica had been interviewed and made the first of four statements on 19 March 1996.

Approximately one year before the murder, Jeanie saw another member of the staff pick up Catherine's knickers and bra from the crib area of the pub. This was in the early morning, as they were cleaning up. A pair of gent's underpants was found beside them. Catherine asked that morning if her knickers and bra had been found, and Jeanie told her that she had found the underpants too. Catherine didn't seem unduly concerned, but instructed that Tom was not to be told.

Jeanie also outlined how she used to bring breakfast up to

Catherine. On one such occasion in the morning, 'I brought up tea to Catherine in the blue room, and I nearly fucking died when I saw Tom Kennedy tucked up in bed with her.'

John Ferguson regularly phoned looking for Catherine, and she would always rush to take the call. Tom and Catherine fought regularly, even up to the time of his murder. She heard Catherine offering to buy out Tom's shares of the pub, but he was having none of it. One of Catherine's favoured verbal attacks during their many rows was: 'Go back to John of God's, you old bastard.' (Tom had been a patient in John of God's in Dublin in relation to his drinking.)

The staff members, young and old, liked Tom Nevin, who had always been kind, considerate and understanding. They were angry at the savage manner in which Tom had been removed from the face of the earth, and anything they could do or say which might assist in righting this terrible wrong would be done by them, even if this meant putting Catherine in the frame.

Elizabeth (Liz) Hudson started work at Jack White's in 1991, worked there for two years, and recommenced work there two and a half years later. On 18 March 1996, she finished work at 12.20 AM; the only people on the premises then were Catherine and Dominic McElligot. As she was getting into the taxi which would take her to Arklow, Tom Nevin was driving two local customers, Johnny Brennan and Frankie Whelan, home. This was a regular occurrence.

As the staff were waiting for the taxi to take them to the disco, someone mentioned about returning as usual to stay at the pub when it was over. Catherine was emphatic, and informed the girls that 'No one is staying at the premises tonight.' Liz told her that she had a key and would let the staff in, to which Catherine replied: 'There's nobody to stay here tonight, end of story.' This was the first such occasion that the staff were refused permission to stay overnight. Earlier, Catherine had told the younger members of the staff getting ready for the disco 'to go up the stairs in pairs and not to make any noise'; no explanation for this request was given.

Liz said that it was usual for Catherine to drink in the course of the day, especially if a person such as Sergeant McElligot was present. That night, however, apart from a drink which she left on the counter, she did not have anything to drink all day. The girls thought this most unusual, as normally she would, after close of business, sit at the counter drinking with a friend or members of the staff. Her one drink remained on the counter with a beer mat on top of it, and strict instructions were issued not to interfere with it.

Liz also said that the frequent guests at the pub included Judge O'Buachalla and Inspector Tom Kennedy. She stated that, in the summer of 1995, Judge O'Buachalla had come in one evening and started drinking with Catherine in the crib area of the pub. They were still there when she was going home. The following morning, Liz saw a lot of empty wine bottles in the crib area, where the two often drank.

Jessica Hunter was employed at the pub up to and including the date of the murder, and stayed in a room a floor above Catherine's. She knew – as did all the other staff members – that Tom and Catherine slept in separate bedrooms. Working with and for Tom was easy and pleasant, but not so for Catherine, whom she described as moody. Catherine, she felt, was very uneasy and edgy the day of the murder, as though she knew that something was going to happen.

Reflecting back on the day of the murder, she felt that Catherine's behaviour was unusual in the extreme and defied logic. Late in the evening, Catherine told her that she was going to check on the clothes in the washing machine. It was Jessica's job to look after and use the machine; she knew this to be a lie, as the machine was broken and couldn't be used.

John Ferguson was also mentioned by Jessica as phoning occasionally looking for Catherine, and especially so a month prior to the murder. On occasions, he phoned twice or three times a day. None of the staff knew who this John Ferguson was.

Catherine was applying pressure on Jessica after making statements to the Gardaí. This came to a head in May 1996, when she walked out. Catherine had intimated to some of the staff that Garda Paul Cummiskey had taken Jessica out to dinner and paid her £35 to make a statement. Catherine would repeatedly say to Jessica: 'Paul is looking for you again to go out for a meal.' This was another figment of Catherine's imagination.

Elaine Butler got a job at Jack White's Inn in June 1995. She got to know Catherine very well – in fact so well that the boss was describing to Elaine intimate details of her marriage with Tom Nevin. Tom, she declared, was an alcoholic, and she was happy that their marriage was over, and that she was no longer married to him. Elaine recalled one morning seeing a large wound on Tom Nevin's forehead, heavily bandaged. Catherine began hassling Elaine after she had made a statement to the Guards, and she left at the end of July 1995.

Alan McGraynor worked as a chef at the pub from 1990 until 20 March 1996, the day he made a statement to the Gardaí. He was one of the longest-serving members of staff, and as such would be familiar with the everyday happenings at the pub. He worked closely with both Tom and Catherine and was trusted by both of them.

Alan would describe the marriage of the Nevins as being primarily business-orientated, with no outward signs of love or affection. He and Tom went on foreign holidays together in 1992 and 1995. He was also aware of telephone calls being received from a John Ferguson, and had no idea who he was, or the purpose of his calls. He said that the front-hallway door was usually mortise-locked. Tom, Catherine and the staff would use the lounge door when they were coming into and leaving the premises. On the night of the murder, the front door was not mortise-locked.

Perhaps the statement taken from Mrs Agnes Phelan, mother of Genesse, who worked at Jack White's up to the date of the murder, most clearly illustrates Catherine's criminal intent towards her husband. At 6 PM on 18 March 1996, Mrs Phelan phoned the pub and informed Catherine that her daughter was ill and unable to work that day. To her dismay, Catherine informed her that she knew about her family problems, and also that her daughter was not sick. Catherine knew that Mrs Phelan had just got back with her husband after being separated for a year, and offered her a solution to the problem: 'You need to sort Walter [her husband] out and throw him out of the house.' She said she was going to 'fucking sort Tom Nevin out'. Some hours later, Tom Nevin, to use Catherine's eloquent English, was 'fucking sorted out'.

Tom Nevin did on occasions drink to excess, and Catherine would have everyone believe that he was a raging alcoholic. Using all her talents of persuasion, as well as her relentless taunting of Tom about him being an alcoholic, Tom ended up as a patient in St John of God's Hospital in Stillorgan, Dublin. Matt Gallagher, a patient there during Tom's stay, recalls Tom and his wife clearly. His account of Catherine makes interesting reading.

He described Tom as a very quiet man, and not very expressive. They became good friends and had many open and frank conversations. On Catherine's visits, he said she treated Tom 'like dirt or a piece of shit'. When she called – and that was seldom – it would be in relation to the business: for Tom to do the books, the VAT returns, and so on. She showed no interest in Tom or his well-being and did not get involved in the family days or the open meetings, though normal procedure dictates that the spouse of a patient should participate.

During one of their conversations, Tom told him that he was happy with the direction the business was taking, but was also convinced that Catherine was trying to get his share of the pub. He was also deeply upset with her sexual activities and was convinced that she was having an affair, stating: 'Anybody could have her but me.' This was in March 1993. It shows how miserable Tom had become with his lot, and that he didn't see any possibility of his marriage ending amicably.

A number of questions had emerged as a result of the interviews with the staff. The identity of John Ferguson remained a mystery. Why was Catherine so insistent that if he phoned, she was to be contacted immediately, regardless of what time it was or what she may be doing? Why did she instruct staff that when she was on the phone to him, they should man the extension? The calls were constant, especially so for a few months prior to the murder, but ceased immediately after it. This man's true identity had to be ascertained, as it was felt that he may have something useful to offer to the investigation.

Catherine's deviousness had been clearly manifested, as were her cunning, temper, sexual encounters and, most of all, her obsessive determination to get Tom out of the business. These were alarming and undisputable facts, but not nearly enough to substantiate the suspicion that she had played some part in the murder of her husband.

15

THE JUDGE

Eyebrows had been raised concerning two acknowledged pillars of the community, Judge Donnacha O'Buachalla, the resident judge for court area number 23, and Tom Kennedy, a former garda inspector; they were, it had been suggested, regular visitors at the pub. Kennedy had been seen in bed with Catherine, and O'Buachalla was regarded by at least one member of staff as being Catherine's boyfriend. At all times, including under oath in the Central Criminal Court, both Kennedy and O'Buachalla denied having a sexual relationship with Catherine.

The frequency with which the judge's name was mentioned in the course of the investigation made it necessary to get a background history on him. Born on 28 March 1945, Judge O'Buachalla is a married man with adult children. The son of a former assistant secretary to the Department of Justice, he worked as a solicitor for the firm Porter Morris in Dublin, having qualified in 1968. He was declared bankrupt in the 1970s and as such his certificate to practice was automatically suspended in 1973, until he discharged the bankruptcy in 1978. His financial investments were the cause of his problems. He was appointed to the Judiciary by the Charlie Haughey-led government in 1989, when Gerry Collins was Minister for Justice. In 1993, he was appointed to District Court number 23, which takes in all of County Wexford, much of County Wicklow and Tullow, County Carlow.

I met Judge O'Buachalla for the first time in 1993, at a District Court sitting in Gorey, where he was the presiding judge. It was not long before we shared a couple of pints after conclusion of the day's business at Gorey District Court. The judge rarely if ever rose for lunch, and as a result the court would normally finish shortly after 1 PM. On the first such occasion, Liam Sexton, the District Court clerk, handed me a note from the judge: 'Pat, will you join me in French's for a pint?' This was to become a fairly regular occurrence.

The judge could fairly be described as easy and pleasant company. In court, he was efficient, didn't like time-wasting, and treated all who appeared before him with dignity and respect. He is an avid golfer, playing off a low handicap. The European Golf Club is a highly regarded course, and was used by O'Buachalla regularly. The club did not have a clubhouse, and Jack White's Inn, which is only a few miles away, became the nineteenth hole. This was a much-needed boost for business at Jack White's. Should there be excessive merriment or drinking, there was no need to chance driving, as the inn had the added bonus of bed-and-breakfast facilities. So popular did Jack White's Inn become with the golfers that many would park in the car park and be driven to and collected from the club by either Tom or Catherine. Like all golf clubs, the European welcomed a judge with open arms. So warm was the welcome, and his presence so desirable, that he was made an honorary life member: not an unwelcomed bonus, considering the fees charged at the club.

His appointment to the bench in 1989 was considered a surprise development by many. Many thought that because he had been declared bankrupt, he could not be considered for appointment to the judiciary. I tried to obtain the name of any other solicitor who had been declared bankrupt and was later elevated to the bench, but it appears that he is the only one. This in no way suggests that his elevation was incorrect; on the contrary, it was correct and lawful. Unusual perhaps, but not sinister or open to question.

The judge and Tom Kennedy developed a close friendship, and both were regular visitors at Jack White's Inn. Tom Kennedy's retirement function, or rather one of them, was held at Jack White's in 1994. It was – surprise, surprise – organised by Catherine, and no effort was spared to ensure that the affection and high esteem in which Kennedy was held in the community was amply demonstrated by a sumptuous retirement party.

The local media were in attendance, as is usual at such functions. Catherine drew up the invitation list, which of course included many politicians, local dignitaries, and Tom's colleagues, past and present. Taking pride of place, and chosen by Catherine to add that extra touch of class, was none other then the local judge. She was later to include amongst her many photographic heirlooms the photograph of his lordship, Tom Kennedy and invited guests at the retirement function. No doubt scant regard was paid to the liquor licensing laws on that particular night of revellery.

Since Tom and Catherine Nevin had taken over in 1986, the pub had gained a reputation for late-night drinking and unusual behaviour; it was generally seen as a place to be given a wide berth. One of the Arklow-based solicitors broached the subject of the judge's visits to the pub, and the gossip circulating about them. I suggested that it was perhaps prudent that one of the local legal profession should inform him about the reputation the pub had gained. To my surprise, the solicitor told me that this had been done, and the judge had responded by telling him that his drinking haunts would be his choice.

Interviewing a judge in the course of a murder investigation is not a task any garda officer would relish. It is not a regular occurrence that a judge is interviewed during a murder investigation, and the media interest could be intense. A garda who was not known locally would do the interview, and Detective Superintendent John McElligot was chosen. The location was the Glenview Hotel, Wicklow. Judge O'Buachalla gave full co-opera-tion and readily made a written, signed statement on 29 April 1996.

He said he had known Tom and Catherine Nevin for more than three years, having been introduced to them by Inspector Tom Kennedy. His relationship with Catherine and Tom was excellent. From time to time, he would rest in the living room, have a shower, let himself out the front door and drive home. He never stayed overnight and never had a key to any part of the premises.

He said that as time passed, he became aware from Tom and Catherine of their great apprehensions, and those of many mem-bers of the local community, in relation to certain local Gardaí. He knew that Tom was greatly troubled by the ongoing matters, and both he and his wife firmly believed that there had been serious garda harassment over the years and that it was futile to make complaints.

Some Gardaí had serious misgivings about bringing cases in front of the judge, and felt that they were not getting fair treatment from him. This unhappy situation came to a head at Arklow District Court in September 1995. Gardaí Whelan and Murphy were but two of the many Gardaí with summary cases listed in their own names that day. I was also present on behalf of the State. The court progressed as usual and Garda Murphy was called to give evidence. The court clerk was instructed by O'Buachalla to admin-ister the oath. There was nothing unusual about that – but what fol-lowed most certainly was. On beginning to give evidence in each new case, O'Buachalla instructed the court clerk to administer the oath on each occasion. The same procedure was insisted on during Garda Vincent Whelan's evidence. All other Gardaí were required to take the oath only once, regardless of the number of cases they had. There was a different procedure being applied to Gardaí Whelan and Murphy, which was both embarrassing and nauseating to me and most Gardaí present.

On conclusion of the court, Murphy and Whelan vented their confusion and outrage to me about the judge's attitude. Some Gardaí suggested that they would never bring cases in front of O'Buachalla again. It was not an easy task to pacify the outraged Gardaí. To a layperson, this may seem a matter of little importance, but to the members of An Garda Síochána present in court that day, it was an uncalled-for deviation from normal practice. All the Gardaí present in court knew that Catherine Nevin had made serious allegations against Murphy and Whelan. They also knew that O'Buachalla was a regular caller to the pub and, on his own admission, enjoyed an excellent relationship with both Tom and Catherine.

I felt that what Judge O'Buachalla did, though unusual, was neither illegal nor a breach of the District Court Rules of 1948. My strict instructions to my staff were: 'Do your job as you have always done; prosecute detections deserving of a court hearing, give your evidence; mission accomplished.' Thankfully, my instructions were heeded.

Increasingly, the national media was taking great interest in Judge O'Buachalla and the gossip circulating about his visits to Jack White's Inn. Catherine's boasts about her ever-increasing friendship with him added greatly to the intrigue. Relations between O'Buachalla and myself took a serious nosedive, and I no longer felt at ease in the judge's company, and certainly not if I was prosecuting when he was presiding.

Our professional and private friendship completely disintegrated around the time I took professional exception to the manner in which he granted the licence for Jack White's Inn on 29 September 1997. I reported what I have always argued, and still maintain, was an incorrect procedure, which I will describe later. Suffice it to say that there were no further invitations to French's pub for pints after conclusion of business at Gorey court. Relations between us were at an all-time low and would remain so until I retired from An Garda Síochána in January 2004. Despite this, I was always impressed with the respect and kindness the judge displayed towards suspects who appeared in front of him.

16

CATHERINE AND THE INSPECTOR

Former inspector Tom Kennedy was another name to be frequently mentioned as a very close associate and confidant of Catherine Nevin. A native of County Kerry, he had an illustrious career in An Garda Síochána before retiring in March 1994. For six or seven years prior to Tom Nevin's murder, he had been frequenting Jack White's Inn and had become very friendly with the Nevins, especially Catherine. She had great confidence in his advice, and even trusted him with making cash drop-offs at the AIB night safe in Wicklow town, where he lived with his wife. Catherine would turn to him for support and guidance arising out of the many alleged burglaries at the pub, such as that involving her wedding ring.

The friendship with Catherine would be described by staff members as sexual. He would at all times deny this, despite the explicit details provided by the young female members of staff. He described Catherine as 'the type of person who would give you a pain in the head when she started getting on about things'. He felt that the situation at Arklow Garda Station was very bad, and that certain people there who enjoyed the hospitality of the Nevins abused it. He admitted preparing insurance claims for Catherine in the past.

Tom Kennedy, in the pre-Catherine Nevin days, could be described as a happily married man, nearing the end of an illustrious career in An Garda Síochána. He is softly spoken, with a bright and keen intellect. All who had served with him held him in high esteem. He was regarded as easy-going and having a very pleasant and friendly manner. But he was also a heavy drinker and it was no secret that his marriage had seen better times – two weaknesses for Catherine to exploit mercilessly.

Many people, in particular locals, found it difficult to understand why an ex-garda inspector was frequenting Jack White's so regularly, as many people regarded the pub as a house that should be given a wide berth. Mrs Kennedy was later to blame Catherine Nevin for destroying their marriage. In an interview, she stated: 'Tom and I are not sleeping together, and we are not even on speaking terms. We are married thirty-four years, and the marriage could have worked. I wanted it to work, I really did, but she, Catherine Nevin, destroyed us. I speak to him only if absolutely necessary. I sleep upstairs and he sleeps downstairs in a little room which he locks, so I can't get in – not that I would want to.' However, it was widely known in Wicklow that the Kennedys' marriage was experiencing difficulties before Tom's liaison with Catherine.

Catherine had on many occasions belittled Tom in public. Why was he prepared to accept this treatment? Why did he stand loyally by her throughout the investigation, and even after she had been charged with the murder of her husband? He wasn't an idiot; far from it. Intimacy, desire, freebies, and perhaps fear of her must be regarded as the reasons Tom Kennedy decided he could not attribute any evilness to Catherine other than: 'She would give me a pain in the head.' This was his only contribution to the murder investigation, after a liaison with her that lasted years. Willie McClean, who admitted to an eighteen-month sexual affair with her, contributed significantly more.

17

THE INJURIES SUSTAINED BY
TOM NEVIN

Prior to Tom Nevin's murder, there were two separate occasions in 1995 when he received injuries during the early hours of the morning at the pub, without satisfactory explanations.

One such incident was on 10 July 1995. Anthony Doyle was driving the ambulance accompanied by James Smullen of Wicklow District Hospital. Tom Nevin was lying on the floor in the pub semi-conscious, with a wound on the top and towards the back of his head. He didn't seem to know anything about the incident or how it had happened: in fact, he said he didn't wish to talk about it.

Doyle saw reading glasses, which were broken, lying some two or three feet from where Tom was lying, and presumed they were his. Tom did not want to go to the hospital, and the ambulance crew had difficulty persuading him to do so. He finally relented and was taken to Casualty at Loughlinstown Hospital.

There was no break-in, and nothing was stolen. Catherine suggested to Gardaí that Tom had fallen when drunk, and had injured himself. They were satisfied that foul play was not an issue.

The second incident happened on 12 October 1995, when

Tom Nevin complained of back pains – a result of falling when getting out of bed. There was a strong smell of drink from his breath; again, he was taken to the Casualty department at Loughlinstown Hospital.

Both injuries suffered by Tom could have been of his own making and perhaps due to drink. There is, however, one puzzling aspect to the head wound sustained by Tom. Catherine told Una Doogue, an employee: 'Tom had been hit during the course of a break-in.' It was also at that time that she was told by Catherine: 'There were two ways Tom Nevin would kill himself, either in the car with drink taken or in the course of a break-in.' Why did she tell Sergeant Daly and Garda Kavanagh that there was no break-in and that Tom's injuries were as a result of a fall by him when drunk?

The murder investigation was moving on to a more critical stage, with Catherine now firmly the main suspect. The team had now reached the stage where they had names of persons whom Catherine had been in contact with, and whom, it was felt, could provide the vital breakthrough.

18

JOHN FERGUSON AND PATRICK RUSSELL

One contact and known confidant of Catherine's was Patrick Russell, of Leixlip, County Kildare. He was arrested on 26 July 1996 for questioning as it was felt that he might have information that could be useful in the investigation.

Born on 18 June 1963, and married with two children, he ran a business trading as Royal Irish Group, in Merrion Square, Dublin. He described himself as an established financial consultant. He was involved with Sinn Féin and, if he had information about the murder, it would be no easy task getting him to part with it. He is highly intelligent, and has no convictions.

There was good reason to believe that he was the person phoning Catherine and using the alias 'John Ferguson'. Enquiries established that he had been in constant contact with her for months prior to, and even up to the week of, the murder. The reasons were unclear, but hopefully would be of benefit in solving the murder.

Pat Russell had all the appearances of a sophisticated and successful businessman. Offices in Merrion Square and an impressive house at Leixlip, County Kildare, were testament to this. He has had dealings with many successful companies both here and in

England. He had a good physique, though was somewhat over-weight. He is always impeccably dressed, usually in expensive designer suits. He is an excellent conversationalist, and more than capable of carrying himself in any company.

Those with the responsibility of interviewing Russell were fully aware of the enormity of the task they faced. It was not unusual in those days, pre-Good Friday Agreement, for members of Sinn Féin to show disdain for, and indeed a lack of co-operation with, An Garda Síochána. The normal approach to arrests and detention by such persons was to pick a spot in the interrogation room, fix eye contact firmly thereon, refuse to answer any questions, and maintain this attitude until their period of detention had expired.

Russell had been arrested by Sergeant Joe O'Hara, who interviewed him, accompanied by Detective Bernie Hanley. Fully aware why he had been arrested, he was quick to point out that he knew nothing about the murder of Tom Nevin. This in itself was of significance: at least he was talking. A number of interviews took place, but he refused to sign any of the transcripts of these interviews when they were read back to him. Eventually, he declared he would make a statement; he did so on 21 July 1996.

He said he knew Tom and Catherine Nevin quite well, having been introduced to them some years previously by John Jones. When he first met them, about ten or twelve years previously, he was a member of Sinn Féin, and a regular visitor to the Sinn Féin advice centre in Finglas. Russell's early involvement with Sinn Féin and the Sinn Féin advice centre continued unabated; in fact, the organisation appointed him chairman of the local cumann. Both Tom and Catherine were also members of the cumann, he stated. After he left the area, he kept in contact with the Nevins; in all, he called to their pub about six or seven times after first making their acquaintance. He was aware that all was not rosy with the Nevins and their marriage.

Shortly after Christmas 1995, Catherine Nevin phoned him at

his office and requested a meeting. She wished to discuss a taxation problem she had. The meeting took place in the Davenport Hotel in Dublin. Her auditors, Coopers and Lybrand, had incurred her wrath by raising an additional invoice of about £2,500, in addition to their annual fee of about £7,000. She also complained to him that they were no longer providing the service they had previously given.

Russell informed her that he was no longer involved in that business and mentioned a firm of accountants, Paffrey Murphy, in Cork. He gave an undertaking to contact them on her behalf and report back to her. She instructed him to be careful when he phoned, as she didn't want the staff or her husband to know what she was doing. She would wait until everything was sorted out before informing Tom about what she was doing.

Concerning the alias he was to use when phoning the pub, he was adamant that the name agreed was 'John Fergus' and not 'Ferguson'. 'Fergus' was the name of his former boss, and the first name he had thought of. Catherine was explicit when telling him: 'When you ring, have no conversations with anyone except me.' If she wasn't there, he was to leave the name 'John Fergus', and she would get back to him.

Having made contact with Noel Murphy of Paffrey Murphy, Russell informed Catherine they were willing to take on the account. An appointment was made for all three – Noel Murphy, Catherine and Russell – to meet in the latter's office. Meetings additional to the one held in Russell's office were held at Nevin's pub, though Russell wasn't sure when, or who was present at them (whether Catherine alone, or both Catherine and Tom). Russell would have got a commission if the contract had gone through. Then, he heard of the murder of Tom Nevin.

Prior to finishing his written statement, he referred back to their meeting in the Davenport Hotel, saying that Catherine had told him she wanted to buy Tom out of the business at Jack White's, but believed that he wouldn't agree.

Russell also supplied some useful information verbally, though this was not included in his written statement. He had heard that Catherine was involved in affairs with other men. He heard rumours that Catherine had put out a contract to have her husband killed in what was to look like a robbery at the pub. When asked about this, he declined to name his informant, but enquiries revealed that John Jones had told Russell that she had approached him about six or seven years previously to carry out the murder. Several people knew about the contract, according to Russell, but he wouldn't name them, and he also felt that they would not cooperate if they were approached.

He knew that Catherine had made an approach to have her husband killed in 1989/90, but Sinn Féin/IRA rejected this approach; she also would have been informed of this. John Jones had contacted him after the murder and sought guidance about going to the Gardaí, as he felt he might be a suspect and wanted to clear his name. Russell advised him to wait until the Gardaí contacted him.

He also knew that Catherine was having affairs – and with whom. He declined to name these individuals; one of them was a personal friend of his, and another he knew from casual meetings they had had.

As a follow-up to Pat Russell's statement, Noel Murphy was interviewed on 14 August 1996. He said that in January or early February 1996, Russell phoned him, saying that he had a potential client, and a meeting was arranged. A meeting took place in Russell's office in late February or early March 1996.

Catherine expressed a desire to change accountants, as she was not satisfied with her present firm. Her husband was not present and she intimated that there could only be an agreement if it was by both of them. Murphy agreed to go to Jack White's Inn sometime in October to meet both Tom and Catherine. A meeting, at which Tom and Catherine were present, took place on 14 March 1996, but nothing definite arose as a result. He tried to phone the pub on 19 March 1996 and got no answer. On phoning Pat Russell, he was informed that Tom Nevin had been murdered that day.

Pat Russell's approach to his arrest and detention was somewhat surprising. Not only was he giving worthwhile information, but he was willing, even eager, to put this in the form of a written statement. As a result of the interviews and written statements made by Russell, many interesting and previously unknown facts concerning Catherine and Tom were ascertained. The phone calls from a 'John Ferguson' she was receiving on a regular basis at Jack White's Inn were in fact made by him, but the name used was 'John Fergus' and not 'Ferguson'. An understandable mistake made by the staff who took the calls.

Pat Russell described Catherine as a 'Clever lassie, I'd say she is ruthless. I wouldn't like to get on her wrong side.'

19

JOHN JONES

John Jones, of Ballbriggan, Dublin, was born on 12 November 1944. From 1984 to 1987, he and Dessie Ellis, of the Provisional IRA, were partners in a television shop, Company Channel Vision, at Church Street, Finglas. This shop doubled as a Sinn Féin advice centre. Ellis was well known nationally, as he had been extradited to England in the late 1980s in connection with bomb-making.

Jones was interviewed on 16 July 1996, and readily admitted that he knew both Tom and Catherine Nevin. Catherine first came to his notice in 1984, when she called to the Sinn Féin advice centre. There were follow-up meetings at the Cappagh House pub in Finglas, which was at the time leased to the Nevins.

He was interviewed again on 27 July 1996 by Sergeant Brian Duffy and Detective Gerry McKenna. He was relaxed and at ease in the presence of the two Gardaí, and had no hesitation in discussing his previous contacts with the Nevins. He volunteered a statement in writing, which was gladly accepted.

At his first meeting with Catherine, she said she had been referred there by a prominent city councillor. Jones was dubious about this information and checked it with the man in question, who could recall no such meeting with her. She was interested in leasing or buying a pub in the area. This type of request was unusual at the centre, and his suspicions were immediately aroused. He later found out that she and Tom had taken over the Barry House pub in Finglas.

Catherine continued to visit the advice centre. Even after buying Jack White's Inn in 1986, she kept in close contact with Jones, and started to visit his home. This was a contact to be cherished and cultivated by her. So intent was she on furthering this friendship that she left a present of meat into his house on one occasion. Jones retained his first impression of her as someone who should be kept at arm's length.

In 1989, Catherine called to the advice centre, and was met as usual by Jones. What she said knocked him for six. Expressionless, she made a proposition: 'She wanted us, Sinn Féin, to stage a robbery, and in the course of it, Tom Nevin, her husband, was to be killed.'

Better – and even more unbelievable – details were to follow: 'The murder should be arranged for the Tuesday following the St Patrick's Bank Holiday weekend. The hit should take place when Tom was en route to the bank, carrying approximately £25,000. The money would be for them.'

Jones didn't quite know what to make of Catherine's proposition, but felt obliged to pass it on to more senior members of Sinn Féin. A meeting was held, and it was decided that this was something to steer clear of. He relayed this information to her, but this did not stop her from making similar approaches. Eventually, he could take no more, and told her never to mention this proposition to him again.

After her last visit to him, he discovered that she had unsuccessfully approached two other members of his organisation with the same proposition. He didn't – or wouldn't – name these people.

Jones heard about Tom Nevin's murder on the news the day it

happened, and alarm bells started ringing in his head. He felt that he knew what had happened, but also had a guilty conscience about what had been proposed to him, and what he should have done about the approach. He was also fearful that Garda enquiries could place him as a potential suspect, if they discovered Catherine had approached him. He turned to Pat Russell, who advised him against going to the Gardaí, as they would, he felt sure, be visiting him in any event.

In his second statement, Jones recalls Catherine calling to the advice centre sporting a black eye and with her wrists bandaged. She stated that this was as a result of a beating at the hands of her husband. That was shortly prior to, or after, her approach to Jones to have Tom murdered. Jones believed that her aim in making the proposition was to get full control of the business.

It was also no coincidence that Catherine told Jones that the hit should take place when Tom was en route to the bank with the lodgement, and after a bank holiday weekend. The takings would be boosted, thus giving an even greater incentive to the hit man.

John Jones and Pat Russell were both shocked at the murder of Tom Nevin, whom they knew and liked. They, or the hierarchy in Sinn Féin, didn't want the organisation's name demeaned by them being cast in the role of hit men operating without a cause, and solely for financial gain.

Catherine had failed miserably in her approaches to Jones. This would perhaps have been sufficient for a lesser individual, but not for Catherine. If she was lacking in anything, it definitely was not confidence in her ability to win over those she needed in any evil adventure she might embark upon – even the murder of her husband.

The plot was getting intriguing, and the finger of suspicion was pointing like an arrow in the direction of Catherine. Nonetheless, she believed that her plans, which she had put together so carefully over a period of years, were flawless.

20

WILLIE MCCLEAN

One valuable find in the search of the pub was the piece of paper with a car registration number written on it. This car turned out to be a Northern-registered Opel Kadett, owned by William McClean's girlfriend of the time. He had a rather flowery past; his self-stated motto was: 'It's only illegal if you're caught.'

In 1990, William McClean visited Jack White's Inn with his girlfriend. Unknown to McClean, Catherine had watched their departure and took note of the registered number of the car they were using. She kept this information until the note was found by Gardaí in the search of the pub. As it transpired, this was another serious blunder by Catherine.

On 3 August 1996, McClean was interviewed by Sergeants Joe O'Hara and Brian Duffy. Far from being shocked, he showed absolutely no surprise on seeing the two, and gave the impression that he was expecting such a visit. Friendly to a fault, he invited his two guests into the house, and was from the outset completely at ease in their company.

Anyone acquainted with McClean would appreciate his penchant for the sensational. Every effort had to be made to keep him focused on the purpose of the visit: what, if anything, did he know about the murder of Tom Nevin? What contacts had he previously had with Catherine, and why did she have the number of his girlfriend's car on a piece of paper? All was to be revealed.

The Red Cow Inn on the Naas Road, Dublin, was a regular watering hole for McClean; he and Catherine had first become acquainted there. Noticing what he would describe as 'a good-looking bird' drinking alone at the bar, he approached her, and was surprised by the pleasant reception he was given. Though not endowed with George Clooney-type looks, he was nonetheless charming, could carry himself well in company, and undoubtedly had the gift of the gab. In fact, one of his friends would state that he suffered from verbal diarrhorea. He made an impression on the lady, who introduced herself as Catherine Nevin. So began an affair – mainly sexual – which was to last for eighteen months. He knew that she was married to Tom Nevin, who at the time was working at Freehill's pub in Dolphins Barn. Their clandestine meetings mostly took place at Tom and Catherine's house in Clondalkin, Dublin, and occasionally in the flats the Nevins owned in Rialto.

McClean became friendly with Tom and was sure that the latter realised what was going on behind his back. When Tom and Catherine bought Jack White's Inn, McClean organised the removal of their furniture. So strong was his friendship with the couple that he was invited to the official opening of the pub. He was a regular there at weekends for the next two or three months.

So brazen and open was the affair that the couple's sexual exploits even took place in the pub. If Tom was ignorant or chose to ignore the obvious, then he was to be hit with the full reality of the situation when he entered Catherine's bedroom one morning. Tom was confronted with the spectacle of Willie and Catherine in bed. To Willie's amazement, Tom just asked where the keys were – to which she replied: downstairs. Tom turned to leave, but not before Catherine had told him: 'The next time you are coming in to my bedroom, fucking knock.' A sense of fear gripped Willie on seeing Tom entering the bedroom. 'Put the shoe on the other foot,' said Willie, 'and I would have been having a go.'

Catherine had become demanding and possessive with her latest conquest – much to his annoyance. He began a cooling-off period, with a view to ending the relationship. Some time later, Willie called to the pub with his girlfriend, hoping that Catherine would at last realise that the affair was finally and irrevocably at an end. Catherine went haywire when she saw his girlfriend, who was a friend of Catherine's from her Dublin days. Another slight snag was the fact that his girlfriend was also married. As the couple departed the pub, Catherine wrote down the number of their car.

The journey back to Dublin was uneventful, but not so what was to greet them at journey's end. The girlfriend's husband was waiting, as was the girlfriend Willie was living with at the time. Catherine had phoned both to have a suitable coming-home party arranged for the two. 'What happened, Willie?' asked Sergeant O'Hara. 'What do you think, Joe?' he replied.

The fact that Willie had a dubious past appealed to Catherine. In 1990, Willie called to Jack White's and Catherine asked him for his phone number. He was surprised, on getting a call some time later from her from St Vincent's Private Hospital, Dublin. She asked him to pay her a visit. When he visited, she explained that the medical problem was to do with her heart. After the customary preliminaries were out of the way, Catherine professed her still-burning love for him and said that she wished to rekindle their affair. He was having none of it, however.

Out of the blue, Catherine asked Willie to do something for her. 'Sure, if possible,' he replied. 'Get rid of Tom and there's £20,000 in it for you.' He was shocked, and not sure whether to laugh or cry. Having regained his composure, he told her in no uncertain terms: 'Fuck off, Catherine.'

Catherine felt sure that she could convince him to carry out the murder. 'You have the contacts. Get him when he is going to the bank or the flats.' As he was leaving the room, he told her: 'No fucking way.' A self-confessed conman, yes, but not a murderer.

The next and last occasion Willie met Catherine prior to the murder was over St Patrick's weekend in 1993, when he called into the pub on his way to Rosslare harbour. The conclusion of his statement is relevant in that he, Willie, shows the trust he placed in Sergeants O'Hara and Duffy: 'I believe that Catherine Nevin really loved me. She never gave me a reason for having Tom done. Well, I never gave her a chance to go into any detail. That's the truth, Joe – I got up and walked out that day.'

Willie McClean used Catherine, and had reaped sexual and other benefits for his efforts. Catherine no doubt tried to use him too, by plying him with drink and sex, but in the end all she really did was put another nail in her own coffin.

21

GERRY HEAPES

On examining Catherine Nevin's diary, seized in the search of the pub on 18 May 1996, it was noticeable that a name and phone number had been scribbled over in an attempt to erase them, on both the front and rear of the page. The name and phone number had been noted by Sergeant Fergus O'Brien and Detective Joe Collins just a couple of weeks after the murder, because the name Gerry Heapes rang a bell with O'Brien.

The phone number was that of one William Adams, of The Ward, County Dublin. Adams ran a warehouse at Kilnamona, The Ward. Some years previously, Heapes had worked for him as a nightwatchman and making deliveries by van. For about nine months, Heapes stayed in a caravan in the yard because of some family problems he was having. Adams had never been in Jack White's Inn, nor did he know the pub's owners. On 28 July 1996, Gerry Heapes was arrested by Detective Sergeant Fergus O'Brien and brought to Enniscorthy Garda Station.

When Heapes was tried and convicted for a robbery at Leydon's cash and carry, he was defended by Paddy McEntee, SC. Their paths would again cross at the trial of Catherine Nevin some twenty years later, but the inimitable Paddy would be doing his damndest to prove that, on this occasion, Heapes's evidence was nothing more than a tissue of lies.

The robbery at the cash and carry could be likened to a comedy of errors. The staff were locked in a room containing a phone. A huge garda squad, both armed and unarmed, surrounded the building. The robbers, active members of Sinn Féin/IRA, panicked, and surrendered. Heapes, on being searched after the arrest, had a sizeable quantity of cash hidden down his pants.

Somewhere along the line, it appears that Gerry Heapes fell from grace with Sinn Féin/IRA – a fact many republicans would confirm. It was also established that the IRA was asked to issue a statement disassociating itself from Heapes – though no such statement was ever issued. It is clear that the organisation did not want to be seen to be getting involved in domestic murders or trials.

On first sight, Heapes is an intimidating figure. He is around six feet tall, very well built, with a huge upper body similar to that of a bodybuilder. On the rare occasions when he laughs, the laugh hardly conceals the permanent scowl he displays. In short, he is not someone to be taking liberties with, or making an enemy of.

It was evident from the moment of the first interview with him that extracting information from him would be extremely difficult. From the point of view of the Gardaí, at least he was talking. As his period of detention increased, so, hopefully, would the quality of the information he was giving. Heapes was aware that his detention could be extended to forty-eight hours. This would pose no problems for him, if he decided to sing dumb.

During the interview, he denied knowing anything about the murder of Tom Nevin, whom he regarded as a friend. The only time he fired a gun was when he was in An Fórsa Cosanta Áitiúil. Yes, he knew Catherine, and had had sex with her once. He knew she was having an affair with 'that chap Willie [McClean]', who had his own room in Jack White's. 'Willie was only interested in drinking all day, and your woman Catherine.' The transcript of this interview, like all the others, was read back to him, and he refused to sign. Eventually, he agreed to make a written statement.

He knew Tom and Catherine when they ran the Cappagh House pub in Finglas, around 1985. He had met Catherine Nevin at the Sinn Féin advice centre. He thought then, and still does: 'She's an evil bitch.' She was hopping in and out of bed with everybody at the time. He had had sex with her once, about two years after they had first met. He was working as a bouncer at the door of the Cappagh White pub, and Catherine, who had moved to Jack White's, called in to the pub and started buying him drink. She got drunk, she brought him back to a flat on the south side of the city, and they had sex. Heapes in fact drove her car there, because of her drunken state. He was invited to the official opening of Jack White's Inn and he stayed overnight, accompanied by his wife.

Around 1990, he entered a pub in North Strand Street, which he knew as Birmingham's. Talk was rife there that Catherine was looking for someone to kill her husband, and was prepared to pay £18,000 for the job.

Not making any secrets about his line of work, he was to elaborate: 'People know me because I make it my business they know me. That is how I earn a living, doing doors around town. It's important that people know me. It was all over the place about Catherine, all the crims had it – that is the heavies, the criminals.'

He attempted to put another man, whom he named to Gardaí, into the frame for the murder. On the morning of the murder, he wasn't sure if he was at home or had driven to Killarney to see his daughter, who worked there. The statement was read back to him but, surprisingly, he refused to sign it.

On 31 July, Heapes returned voluntarily to Enniscorthy Garda Station and intimated that he wished to make a full and detailed statement about his dealings with Catherine Nevin. He gave as a reason for refusing to sign his first statement his desire to consult his organisation first.

Some years after the official opening of Jack White's, he met

Catherine in Finglas. She was driving a big white car. She asked him to accompany her for a spin. She complained that Tom was making her life hell, beating her up and having affairs. The money to buy Jack White's Inn had been hers, and Tom hadn't contributed, she said. Heapes listened to this with amusement and incredulity. He had come to regard her as a dangerous and compulsive liar.

Suddenly, like a bolt from the heavens, she faced him and calmly asked: 'Would you get rid of him?' She wanted Tom shot dead. This was no wind-up, he realised, but deadly serious stuff. He told her: 'That would cost a lot of money.' Retaining her icy composure, she insisted that money would not be a problem, because on a bank holiday weekend, Tom would be carrying between £20,000 and £25,000 to lodge in the bank. He told her to leave it with him and to get back to him in a week or two.

Heapes, still shocked at Catherine's proposal, believed that the matter was so serious that it would have to be passed on to 'his people', as he put it, for consideration and determination. He was instructed to get as much detail from her about her plan to have her husband killed as possible.

A few weeks later, Catherine arranged a meeting. The proposition she had previously made was quickly resurrected, and a definite answer demanded. Gerry told her that no one would take on such a job for the amount of money she was offering. Undeterred, she explained that there was a double insurance policy on Tom's life and that she would pay him after the money had been collected. Not good enough, he told her; there had to be money up front.

Two or three weeks later, Catherine had devised a new plan, which involved skimming money out of the takings at the pub each week. She would open an account in her maiden name, Scully, and Tom would be unaware that money was disappearing. 'Get back to me,' Heapes told her, 'when the money is in the account.'

Some four or five weeks later, in the Phoenix Park, Catherine produced a bank book with lodgements in it, and showed him a name in it he took little notice of, but which was, she stated, her maiden name. Realising that Catherine was utterly determined, he decided to play along. 'How should it be done, Catherine?' he asked.

Catherine then drove to South Circular Road and stopped outside a house, where she informed him: 'This is Tom's first stop after he leaves Jack White's. There is usually a barman or a handyman in the car with him. The passenger would enter their properties and collect the rent, leaving Tom alone in the car. What better place to do it?'

Heapes made excuses about the location: the streets were too narrow, with too many cars parked on them, some with occupants. She then suggested waiting for him inside the house, and to 'do' him as he entered. Not a runner, he told her; come up with a better idea.

Three days later, another meeting took place. This time the chosen route was from South Circular Road to Islandbridge, and into Phoenix Park. This was, she stated, the route Tom always took to the bank; if he hadn't arrived at the bank by lunchtime, he would have driven to Clonee, and parked directly outside a window at the Grasshopper pub. Leaving the takings in the car boot with the alarm switched on, he would take his usual place, which afforded a view of his car from his table. After lunch, he would return to Blanchardstown and stop at the Kepak factory to collect meat for the pub. The Grasshopper pub was the perfect location for the hit, according to Catherine.

She drove to a location with a view of Islandbridge, and the road coming from their flats. Tom's car, on its normal route, could be seen from this vantage point and could be easily followed to Clonee. Money was discussed: Catherine suggested £35,000, of which £10,000 would be paid up front and the remaining £25,000 handed over after the job had been successfully completed.

Heapes's organisation wasn't pleased with Catherine's continued pursuit of her objective. He got the impression that they would stop her either by telling Tom about her plans, or calling Catherine to one side and informing her of their views.

Catherine's pursuit of her goal was relentless: another meeting took place a few days later. They drove to the Grasshopper pub in Clonee, and stopped outside it. She referred to her lack of an acceptable alibi – a subject to which she had given much thought and consideration. She would make sure that Tom would be accompanied by her and would then follow his normal routine by going to the Grasshopper pub for lunch. Being with Tom as he was shot would give her the perfect alibi. It would be all the better if she was wounded, as she would really look the part of the grieving widow. Heapes tried to put her off by saying that the plan was too dangerous, because when the shooting started there was no telling where the bullets would fly. She was having none of it.

Just how was he to get possession of the keys of Tom's car (where the money was locked in the boot), he asked. Catherine, as usual, had the answer. 'Tom would have the keys in his hand as he exited the pub, and when he was shot they could be taken. He couldn't do anything about it as he would be dead.' That St Patrick's weekend would be ideal, she suggested. Heapes once more baulked, telling her that he needed more time to prepare.

This latest meeting had really shaken Heapes, and he decided that enough was enough. His organisation told him that something was being done straight away about Catherine. Some days later, he heard that people had told Catherine that they knew what she was up to. If they heard she was making an approach to anyone else to have Tom Nevin murdered, they would inform Tom and deal with her, plus anyone she had been in contact with. That was the last contact Catherine had with Heapes for a few years.

Pierce Moran's statement was regarded as crucial in proving the account as given by Heapes. Moran was a long-time friend of Heapes. They decided to visit Jack White's pub in late January or early February 1994, intent on conning Catherine out of £10,000.

Heapes had briefed Moran on her previous attempts to get him to murder her husband.

Heapes would introduce Moran to Catherine, and Moran would then absent himself for a few minutes. During his absence, Gerry would explain Moran's credentials as a hit man par excellence, who was prepared to bump off Tom for her original offer. It seemed easy enough, they thought: they would get the £10,000 and pocket it. They had no intention of going through with the murder. Catherine couldn't report the incident to the Gardaí, so there was no apparent risk involved.

From his many previous dealings with Catherine, Heapes should have known better. They entered the pub, and Catherine immediately joined them. She put up free drinks and meals, took Heapes to one side and told him: 'Things are fine again between Tom and myself, I no longer want him killed.' 'The bitch smelt a rat,' exclaimed Heapes. 'She was trying to convince us she was still heeding the warning about trying to get Tom murdered.'

Several of Heapes's disclosures were corroborated. Verification of the white car came from Hill's Garage, Arklow. Tom Nevin bought a white Opel Vectra from Hill's on 3 January 1989, and retained it until 5 September 1990. This would cover the period Catherine and Heapes were meeting and undertaking the journeys outlined above.

Catherine told Heapes there were two insurance policies on Tom's life. The Gardaí verified an ordinary life policy taken out on 1 May 1983, by Catherine, which shows 'Catherine Nevin' as the beneficiary. This policy was valued at £77,874 in 1996. The second was a mortgage-protection policy with the Irish Progressive Life Assurance, and it insures the lives of Tom and Catherine Nevin for £300,000 each.

A bank book was found at the pub, showing details of an Allied Irish Bank deposit account in the name of 'Catherine Scully', with an address c/o AIB, Lower Drumcondra Rd, Dublin 9. The Gardaí are satisfied that this account was originally opened at the Blanchardstown branch on 23 June 1989.

An employee who travelled with Tom to the bank verified Heapes's account of the route travelled by Tom, and as indicated to him by Catherine.

At one meeting, Catherine Nevin said: 'St Patrick's weekend would be the ideal time to do it.' St Patrick's Day fell on a Friday in 1989, leading to an extended bank holiday weekend. Coincidentally, the murder of Tom Nevin was also committed on an extended St Patrick's weekend in 1996.

Gerry Heapes could not be in possession of these details had they not been imparted to him by Catherine Nevin. Heapes's wife surely had a relevant and significant input into his decision to return voluntarily to the station. She had endured enough during previous years, especially for the botched robbery at Leydon's cash and carry. She wanted no more trouble from the Gardaí or anyone else, and implored him to cooperate.

His cooperation included an offer to take the Gardaí on a guided tour of all the locations which had been pointed out to him by Catherine. Billy Randle, who invariably accompanied Tom on his weekly trips to these locations, verified them. The Grasshopper pub in Clonee and the Kepak meat factory would have been known only to him, Catherine and Tom. Catherine strenuously denied supplying this detailed information to Heapes.

22

CATHERINE'S ARREST

The decision to arrest Catherine Nevin was carefully considered. Picking an opportune time and date to arrest a person in connection with a murder is dependent on whether enough relevant information has been unearthed to justify a file being sent to the Director of Public Prosecutions. Some Gardaí felt that without Catherine coming clean, the chances of convincing the DPP to proceed were slim in the extreme.

Others felt that highly significant evidence, albeit much of it circumstantial, had been unearthed. This word 'circumstantial' was to be a key factor. There was nothing to suggest that Catherine had pulled the trigger to discharge the fatal shot into the chest of her husband. It was not necessary that this could, or should, be proven against her to justify a charge of murder. If her conspiracy with others, or her approaches to other people prior to the murder, were to be proven in a court of law, she would be equally guilty as the person who actually shot Tom Nevin.

It is perhaps necessary to explain in some detail Section 30 of the Offences against the State Act 1939. This was the section relied upon by the Gardaí in making arrests and detaining for questioning suspects in connection with specified serious criminal cases, including murder.

Section 30 provided an initial detention period of twenty-four hours, followed by an additional period of another twenty-four hours if this was authorised in writing by an officer not below the rank of chief superintendent.

Before an arrest under the Offences against the State Act 1939, the particular crime had to be included under the schedule of offences listed in the Act: Offences under Malicious Damage Act 1861, Offences under Explosive Substances Act 1883, Offence under Firearms Act 1925/90 and Offences against State Acts 1939/90, Sections 6, 7, 8, 9 and 12.

Reliance on Section 30 has posed many difficulties for the Gardaí on occasions, not least of which was the arrest and detention of suspects for murder. The power of arrest posed no problems, but a problem would occasionally arise in the detention of the suspect. The actual act of murder was not included in the schedule of offences under the Offences against the State Act, so invariably the Firearms Act is availed of. I am aware of an instance in which the culprit had used a bread knife – the property of the victim – to inflict the fatal wound in the course of a burglary. In the attack, the knife broke, thereby creating the offence of Malicious Damage and giving the Gardaí the power of detention under the Offences against the State Act 1939. Such were the constraints imposed by our legislators in the ongoing fight against crime and criminals. Thankfully, the Gardaí now have much greater powers of detention after arrest.

The team felt that they had taken the investigation as far as possible, and it was now time to put Catherine's protestations of innocence to the test. The order was given to arrest her. Sergeant Joe O'Hara was selected for the task. At 8.20 PM on 27 July 1996, O'Hara arrived at Jack White's pub. To his surprise, the media were already there, perhaps as a result of a tip-off or, more likely, due to good investigative work by the media.

Catherine didn't go into shock or throw a tantrum when she was arrested. As she was entering the garda car, she shouted to one of her staff: 'Contact my solicitor.' The arrest took place on the roadway outside the pub – much to the delight of the photographers. The incident was splashed across the newspapers the following day. The journey from Jack White's pub to Enniscorthy Garda Station was uneventful, as Joe tried unsuccessfully to engage Catherine in conversation. Was this to be a taste of what was to follow? Her first interview would reveal how she intended to approach the situation.

Catherine had told Detective Sergeant O'Brien and Detective Collins of her dislike and distrust for all the Arklow Gardaí, myself in particular. Detective Sergeant J. Healy and Sergeant O'Connor, based in Dublin, had no past history at Jack White's Inn, or with Catherine Nevin. So surely she could, and would, have confidence in them. Was she not eager to bring to justice the perpetrators of this ghastly crime?

At 9.20 PM, O'Connor and Healy were sitting opposite Catherine Nevin in the interview room at Enniscorthy Garda Station. They introduced themselves and explained that they believed she could assist them in relation to the murder of her husband. She was given the usual legal caution. The only words spoken by Catherine Nevin were: 'I want my solicitor, Donacha Lehane.' She supplied his phone number, but there was no reply when he was phoned. At 10.05 PM, Catherine requested a doctor, and medication. The doctor arrived at 10.20 PM and left twenty minutes later. She was placed in the cell at 11.56 PM and questioning was suspended for the day. She had said nothing while being questioned.

From an investigative point of view, the first interview was to unleash a bag of mixed feelings for the interrogators. It was abundantly clear that Catherine had anticipated her arrest. Advice would have been given to her by her solicitor that she had the right to remain silent. Knowing that the choices open to her were lim-

ited, she would have to determine in advance whether to cooperate – or at least try to give that impression – or, alternatively, to
'sing dumb'.

Her choice of action has to be viewed as an enormous mistake. If she had nothing to hide, why not co-operate? Her attitude
and behaviour was more akin to that of a terrorist than to a grieving wife. It was still early in her detention, and the hoped-for
change of heart might just happen. Detective Sergeant Fergus
O'Brien and Detective Joe Collins were the most likely to accom-
plish this. They had played a huge part in the investigation so far,
and were the people who were mainly responsible for putting John
Jones, William McClean, Gerry Heapes and Pat Russell (alias John
Ferguson) into the frame as people who could, and hopefully
would, supply information relevant to the investigation.

Both have unique and perhaps even similar talents in the art of
eliciting information from suspects. O'Brien, a former rugby back-
row forward of note, stands well over six foot tall and is built to
proportion. His smile includes a set of teeth which could be used
to advertise toothpaste. He has a very pleasant personality, and the
old saying 'He could charm the cross off an ass' definitely applies
to him. Collins does not have the same imposing physique as
Fergus, but is nonetheless very charismatic. His interviewing techniques were once described by someone on the receiving end of
them as: 'If that fella asked you what you had for breakfast, not
alone would he get the answer, but also what you had for dinner
as well.'

'Well, Catherine, how are things going?' came the opening
salvo from Joe. 'Catherine, we are here to help you. Let's talk, and
give us the story as it happened. You are doing yourself no favours
by not talking. After all, if you have nothing to hide, why the
silence?' The hoped-for breakthrough was not happening – if her
expression of contempt and arrogance was a barometer of intent.
This joust had a total of forty-eight hours to run. During that
time, she would be given every possible opportunity to tell her

story – or indeed any story. She chose to take a vow of silence.

The interview commenced at 8.21 AM the next morning and concluded two hours later. Catherine did not answer a single question and refused to sign the notes afterwards. This was typical of all interviews conducted with her during the period of her detention.

Catherine made a number of complaints concerning alleged mistreatment during her period of detention. Peter Creane, an Enniscorthy-based solicitor, acted briefly for Catherine during her detention. On the afternoon of the 28 July, Creane said he wanted to enter into the custody record that the prisoner had stated that the line of questioning was abusive and threatening. That night, Catherine handed Garda Ann Shore two prepared written statements. Her solicitor, Garret Sheehan (who had not been available previously), was present. In one statement, she complained that she had been continously questioned about the murder of her husband Tom, and that she had already made a full statement to the Gardaí and had nothing further to say. In the second statement, she said that she had been frequently subjected to serious insult and verbal abuse by the Gardaí. On 29 July, at 4.50 PM, Catherine Nevin requested that Sheehan be informed that she had been assaulted by Sergeant O'Hara. Her complaints were forwarded to the Garda Complaints Board, who vindicated the good name of Sergeant Joe O'Hara, and all others involved in Catherine's questioning.

Prior to her release, Catherine was asked to sign the custody record, and was asked if she had any complaints. She said: 'I will sign nothing.' She did not make any complaints at that time.

The possibility that Catherine or her legal representatives might make an issue about the interviewers being exclusively male was considered, and she was given an opportunity to tell her story to female Gardaí. Detective Sergeant Noreen O'Sullivan and Garda Margaret Howard, both Dublin-based (Catherine had refused to speak to local Gardaí), were chosen. The result was the same as it had been for their male colleagues: Catherine refused to answer questions or to sign the notes of the interview. Even the meals supplied to Catherine were refused by her.

She was released at 8.09 PM on 29 July, and was met by a horde of photographers. There was no joy for them: she didn't say a word. At the brief news conference which followed, I faced a barrage of questions from the assembled media.

'Was she charged, and if not, will she be charged?'

'No, she was not, and a charge, if any, will be a decision taken not by myself, but by the Director of Public Prosecutions.'

'Is a file being sent to the Director of Public Prosecutions, and if so what recommendations will it contain?'

'Yes, eventually a file will be sent to the DPP, and hopefully in the near future. At this stage it is too early to give firm indications as to the recommendations that will be included in it.'

'When is it expected that the investigation will be concluded?'

'It is not known, but the sooner the better.'

'Do you expect a charge as a result of the investigation?'

'Yes.'

'Against whom?'

'Not yet in a position to say.'

I then brought the interview to a close – much to the annoyance of the reporters.

Catherine must have felt satisfied with her performance during her detention – which, she confided to friends, was a big mistake by ourselves. 'Why weren't they arresting and charging the murderer, rather than wasting valuable time in arresting the last person who wanted or wished Tom Nevin dead?' she said after her release. Her day was coming, she told them confidently. Yes it was, but not as she would have envisaged.

Back at the pub, she put on a brave face. In the meantime, business had, if anything, improved – driven mainly by curiosity about recent developments. Customers wanted to get a glimpse of Mrs Nevin, the unfortunate and harshly treated wife of the murdered Tom Nevin. Women had never frequented the pub in large numbers, even prior to the murder, but since the murder no women went there at all. Now that she had been arrested and questioned in connection with the murder of her husband, Catherine's standing locally, even nationally, took a serious nose-dive. She was now regarded by the public, perhaps for the first time, as a real suspect.

The next meeting of significance with Catherine took place at Jack White's Inn on 4 December 1996. O'Brien and Collins, the two detectives she had reposed such confidence and trust in, paid her a visit at the pub to put to her the allegation that she had solicited the murder of her husband Tom. It was imperative that she should be given an opportunity to respond.

Catherine was sitting at the counter in the company of former inspector Tom Kennedy, both apparently without a care in the world. This was eight months after Tom Nevin's murder; Kennedy was well aware that she had been arrested, and questioned as a suspect.

Collins asked if they could speak to her in private, but was told that she was happy to speak to them in the presence of Kennedy. He was also at ease, and happy to stay by her side. There had been serious allegations made against her, Joe stated, and he explained that a number of men had described how she had approached them on different occasions, and propositioned them to kill her husband. This was expected to take her by surprise, but instead she rose from her seat, her facial expression unchanged, walked to the counter and, without uttering a syllable, wrote on a piece of paper the name and phone number of her solicitor.

Collins rather sheepishly asked the obvious: 'Does this mean you do not wish to comment on the allegations?' Swift and clear came the reply: 'Yes, thank you very much, see my solicitor.'

Had Tom Kennedy taken leave of his senses? He had stayed faithful to her after she had been arrested and questioned as a suspect, for the murder of her husband. Now he was sitting by her side and listening to Joe Collins – whom he knew well, and who had been his boss occasionally – telling Catherine that he had information suggesting that she had approached various men to have her husband murdered. His reactions were completely indifferent, as if Collins had said: 'Terrible day Catherine, it's definitely a day for the high stool.' Everyone was asking why he was remaining so loyal to her.

23

STOCKTAKE

Tom's realisation of the marital predicament in which he found himself is best summed up by Catherine's aunt, Patricia Flood, who had a visit from him around Christmas 1994. During their conversation, he confided his feelings to her. He started to cry and, putting his hands over his face, said: 'You don't know what I have to put up with, you don't know the half of it. How would you like to see Tom Kennedy coming out of Catherine's room in the morning?' This shocked Patricia. She said to him: 'Is she trying to drive you mad? Is there any way out, take half and get out?' He didn't think he could. He gave the impression that he was afraid of her, and was even afraid to talk about the situation too much. Catherine never tried to conceal her contempt and hatred for Tom Nevin. Her public outbursts towards him were not the usual marital squabbles.

She had meetings with Anthony Morrissey, an auctioneer; although he was not called as a witness, he supplied valuable information. On 31 January 1990, Catherine Nevin contacted him to do a valuation of the pub. He visited it on 15 February, and discussed various matters, including the market price, and how the pub would be sold. Catherine told him that Coopers & Lybrand accountants would supply figures for the pub, but they never arrived at his office.

The next contact was when a 'Mr Kennedy' phoned his office on behalf of Catherine Nevin, on 14 October 1992. Kennedy asked someone from the firm to visit the pub; Morrissey's father and brother did so the following day. Catherine alone was present, and she told them that she was in negotiations with Maxol Oil Company for the purchase of the pub. If a reasonable offer was made, she would sell it. After that, there was no further communication until 29 July 1993, when Catherine phoned saying that she had done a deal on a pub in Dublin and wanted to sell Jack White's. A meeting was arranged for 4 August 1993. No one else was present – certainly not her husband.

At Catherine's behest, the next meeting took place on 18 September 1993. Morrissey and Catherine had a lengthy discussion, and he took various measurements and the usual matters associated with the intended sale of a property were discussed. At a later date, Morrissey did a valuation of the two houses at 6 Mayfield Road and 18 Mountshannon Road, Dublin.

The significance attaching to the meetings was Catherine's intentions, even as late as 22 April 1996, to sell their properties, pub and houses alike. Tom Nevin was unaware of her attempts to sell the pub behind his back. But not so the other Tom, described by Morrissey as 'heavily built with grey hair'. Morrissey was informed by one of the staff that his name was Tom, and he was a garda by profession. This clearly illustrates Catherine's scheming and secretive attempts to sell the pub as far back as January 1990.

Catherine's arrest should have hit home, and made her realise that the time had come to play ball and co-operate. She had decided on the course of action she would adopt during her forty-eight-hour period of detention. Not alone would she refuse to answer even the most rudimentary questions, but she would try to blacken the character of Sergeant Joe O'Hara by making a false claim that he had physically assaulted her during an interview.

It was felt by all members of the investigation team that it was of paramount importance that the DPP should be satisfied that the disclosures of Messrs Gerry Heapes, John Jones and William McClean were reliable. This might take some achieving, having regard to their criminal records, and the fact that Gerry Heapes had been involved with the IRA. However, their stories were so similar that they could not have been concocted in such fine and similar detail by all three: they must have come from Catherine's lips.

On the minus side, all three had a criminal past – the most serious of which was the armed robbery recorded against Gerry Heapes. Of significance also was the fact that, of the three, he was the only one who had not signed his written statement.

All three men had shown a willingness to assist in the investigation. Heapes was perhaps the most reluctant of the three, but then he had by far the most sinister past, and the most reason to be apprehensive.

Would the case ever have gone to court without the evidence of the three? The answer has to be a definite no. Perhaps it would have done on a lesser charge than would be recommended to the DPP, but certainly not for 'murder' or 'soliciting murder'.

Speculation was rife amongst the public, and of course the media, regarding the likelihood of Catherine Nevin being charged with her husband's murder. By the time the file which had been so expertly prepared by Detective Sergeant Liam Hogan was submitted to the DPP, she had been firmly entrenched in the minds of practically everyone as not alone the chief suspect, but the culprit.

Such was the intense interest in the investigation by the media and public alike that it was virtually impossible for any member of the investigation team to socialise. Invariably, some person would approach offering advice, giving their views and opinions. I had given strict instructions from day one that there would be no disclosure of any information that might impinge upon the success of the prosecution. Despite protestations later, at the trial, of

Gardaí leaking information, relevant material was definitely not divulged.

The file was submitted and the DPP's directions eagerly awaited. Several meetings took place with staff from the DPP's office to clarify ambiguities and discuss the likely attitudes of Heapes, Jones and McClean if they were called upon to give evidence in a court of law.

24

THE DIRECTOR OF PUBLIC PROSECUTIONS

Finally, in the second week of April 1997, a little more than a year after the murder was committed, the DPP's directions were received: 'Prosecute Catherine Nevin, on one count of murdering her husband Tom Nevin, and three separate counts of soliciting his murder.'

There was unrestrained joy at this development, which was an acknowledgement of all the long hours, days and months the investigation team had put in. However, the joy was tempered to some extent by the knowledge that this was only the first obstacle cleared.

Catherine's movements on 14 April 1997 were closely monitored, as it had been decided to arrest and charge her on that date. Detective Sergeant O'Brien and Detective Pat Mulcahy were chosen for this task. Catherine, when driving through Ballybough, Dublin, was stopped by O'Brien, who informed her that she was being arrested for the murder of, and for soliciting the murder of, her husband Tom Nevin. She made no reply, but looked incredulously at him. The person she had reposed such respect and confidence in was now arresting her. For the first time since the murder, she seemed to display a sense of shock at this unexpected development. Maybe the realisation hit her that her meticulously and deviously conceived plan to murder her husband was not as perfect as she had believed.

I was also present as Catherine was placed into the garda car to be taken to the Bridewell Garda Station for charging, and I felt an enormous sense of achievement. What had been unearthed in the course of the investigation was mostly circumstantial evidence. That alone would be insufficient, if it was not added to significantly by other evidence. Most importantly, three men whom Catherine had propositioned to murder her husband had made written statements to the Gardaí and were prepared to give evidence at the trial.

Generally speaking, circumstantial evidence may be included under the headings of motive, preparation, opportunity and subsequent conduct. In a case of murder, for example, each of the following would be circumstantial evidence: the fact that the accused bore ill will against the deceased; the procurement of a weapon before the crime was committed; being seen in the vicinity shortly before or after the crime; hiding the instrument with which the crime was committed; possession of stolen property; absconding; and so on. The Court of Criminal Appeal has decided that there may be a combination of circumstances, no one of which would raise a reasonable conviction, or more than mere suspicion, but which, taken together, may create a conclusion of certain guilt.

Catherine was remanded in custody but a few days later was granted bail in the High Court. Not surprisingly, media interest was at fever pitch, and coverage of developments was intense. The country was enthralled with the latest developments.

An early hearing was never a runner: all the higher courts have huge waiting lists, in particular the Central Criminal Court. The case was listed to commence on 12 January 2000. The presiding judge would be Ms Mella Carroll: her father was a past commissioner of An Garda Síochána.

Catherine was the most talked-about woman in Ireland. Wherever she went, her presence caused huge interest and generated gossip. Her photograph had appeared in all the national and local newspapers. In the immediate aftermath of the murder, she had been portrayed as the shocked and grief-stricken widow. One such photograph at her husband's funeral showed her holding a single red rose to her face when standing by the graveside. Now sympathy was being replaced slowly but surely by suspicion. Gossip did not confine itself to Catherine alone. Judge Donnacha O'Buachalla and former garda inspector Tom Kennedy were also drawn into the web of intrigue.

25

THE TRIAL

The commencement of Catherine Nevin's trial generated unprecedented interest among the media and public. It was nearly four years from 19 March 1996, when Tom Nevin had been murdered. His wife Catherine now faced a jury of her peers, charged with his murder and three separate counts of soliciting William McClean, Gerry Heapes and John Jones to have him murdered. The courtroom was packed to capacity; even standing room was limited, and only available to those who had waited patiently for hours in the hope of gaining admittance. If those present expected to see a broken, miserable woman, they were sorely disappointed: Catherine had a steely determination to emerge unscathed, a winner in every sense.

The legal teams, both defence and prosecution, were rightly regarded as amongst the best in the land. Mr Peter Charlton SC, assisted by Mr Tom O'Connell BL, were the prosecuting team. Michael Kennedy was representing the Chief State Solicitor's office. Mr Charlton is instantly recognisable in court because of the fact that he does not wear a wig. He lectured in law at Trinity College and is the author of much-used law textbooks. He is also an accomplished pianist and had to make a choice between law and music as a career.

The defence team was headed by no less a personage than the inimitable Mr Paddy McEntee SC, ably assisted by Mr Paul Burns BL and instructed by Garret Sheehan, solicitor. Mr McEntee is arguably the best-known barrister in the state. His expertise and abilities are legendary. He has represented many persons accused of some of the most notorious and heinous crimes ever committed in this country. Dominic McGlinchy and Malcolm McArthur immediately spring to mind.

Judge Mella Carroll had a spectacular and meteoric rise to her present position. As a barrister, she specialised in company law. She was the first woman to head the Bar Council and the first woman to be appointed a High Court judge.

The would-be jurors were packed like sardines into the confines of the courtroom, anxiously awaiting the result of the draw which would determine the part, if any, they would play in determining the guilt or innocence of Catherine Nevin. They were not there by choice, but as a result of a summons to attend for jury service. Those chosen would come to regard themselves as the unlucky ones, and would have their normal, everyday activities seriously curtailed for the duration of the trial.

26

PRE-TRIAL ARGUMENTS

Pre-trial arguments are not unusual in serious cases, and this was to be no exception. Paddy McEntee protested that the murder charge should be separated from the soliciting charges. Better was to follow, when he asked Judge Carroll to stop the trial, as pre-trial publicity would have a prejudicial effect on the jury, all of whom would have seen the coverage. Paddy McEntee also stated: 'I am seeking discovery of Special Branch files on the main prosecution witnesses, John Jones, Gerry Heapes, William McClean and Pat Russell.'

Media coverage, Mr McEntee submitted, could prove adverse to the interests of his client. He made reference to an article in the *Evening Herald* which, he suggested, was calculated to portray Mr Nevin as a simple, gormless country boy and Catherine as a sophisticated Dub. Judge Carroll dismissed the article as having no prejudicial effect. However, she directed the jury not to read newspaper reports, or listen to or see radio and TV coverage of the trial for its duration. On 21 January, Mr McEntee again voiced objections about media coverage, mentioning in particular the *Evening Herald* and *Irish Independent*. He took exception to comments on Catherine's choice of clothes, hairstyle and reading material. He also took exception to the press referring to her as 'the Black Widow'. He suggested that all of this was designed to dehumanise Catherine and turn her into nothing more than a sex object. On 1 February, he stated: 'I am now seeking an adjournment and, if the judge refuses, would be forced to renew my application for a permanent stay.'

Mr Peter Charlton responded by submitting that while he accepted that such references were deeply discourteous and at times offensive, the evidence fell short of the defence claim of a deliberate attempt to 'get at' the jury. The next day, Judge Carroll refused the application. She described the colour pieces as the worst kind of tabloid journalism, designed to sell newspapers, without regard to Catherine's dignity as a human person. 'I do not subscribe to the view she had been deliberately demonised. She is entitled to wear in court what she likes without being dissected.'

Refusing to defer the trial, she ordered: 'Until this trial is finalised, there should be no further comment on Mrs Nevin's dress, hairstyle, nail varnish or reading material. No further photographs of her are to be published in the press until the trial is over. If there is a repetition or attempts to photograph her, application can be made to me.' The prohibition on pictures did not extend to TV, and images of her were also carried on many websites.

A number of prominent journalists, most of whom were crime reporters, were called concerning their coverage of events, and information allegedly leaked to them by Gardaí. Liz Allen, of the *Sunday Independent*, confirmed that: 'No statement had been supplied to me by the Gardaí', while Stephan Rea, of the *Evening Herald*, said that he found the police in this case to be most unhelpful in his enquiries. The judge refused the applications to stop the trial.

On 25 February 2000, the media once more came in for some stick, this time from Mr Charlton. He referred to an error in an *Irish Times* report, in which 'one of the men's fingerprints was found at the scene of the crime' appeared instead of 'none'. Mr

Charlton was infuriated and expressed his outrage at such a 'sinister error'. He called on the editor to print a front-page apology and to report what actually goes on in court for a change. Mr McEntee was not sitting idly by during Peter Charlton's outburst, and joined in the condemnation – though why is not readily understood. McEntee called the piece of journalism 'as gross a bit of misreporting as one could conceive of, I dare not say my lord, but it is my duty to ask the court to discharge the jury'. This latest application by McEntee brought quiet laughter from many of those in attendance. God loves a trier.

At this stage, counsel for Heapes, Jones and McClean sought an interim order prohibiting the press from improperly describing his clients. The judge consented, and ruled: 'The right of freedom of expression does not include the right to publish untrue statements about any witness.' She banned the newspaper groups concerned, Independent Newspapers and the Trinity Mirror Group, from making anything other than factual reports. She also banned the publication of statements (if any) made by the IRA, confirming or denying that Tom Nevin was a member of that organisation.

There was still more to come, and on 10 March, Mr McEntee once more applied for the jury to be discharged. The *Evening Herald* had issued an article profiling Judge Donnacha O'Buachalla. Judge O'Carroll ordered the editor, Gerry O'Regan, to be brought before her. O'Regan attended court but was not called on to give evidence. Judge Carroll asked counsel for the *Herald*: 'If the trial had to be aborted, how would your client like to have to pay for the costs to date?' Counsel replied: 'There has been no deliberate attempt to frustrate the trial.' The judge responded that she was coming to the view that, in a criminal trial, the reporting should be limited to what happens in court and nothing else. She added: 'I have never known a trial where there has been as much intrusion by the newspapers . . . a fair trial comes before the rights of the mass media to make money.'

The following day, Judge Carroll dismissed all of the defence applications. All four counts should proceed jointly; Catherine Nevin would receive a fair trial. She further ruled that the suggested leaking of information by the Gardaí was 'a bit far-fetched'.

Throughout the arguments, Catherine sat impassively and displayed her expertise as a tutor of deportment and dress. She was immaculately attired in designer clothes, and adorned in many items of what appeared to be expensive jewellery. This display would continue throughout the sixty days of the trial. She gave the impression of being completely composed.

On 14 January 2000, the charges were put to Catherine Nevin; she pleaded not guilty to all four. However, the issue of the Special Branch files on McClean, Jones, Heapes and Russell had not gone away. Charlton asserted that this was the first time in the history of the state that Special Branch files had been sought in a murder prosecution. This was causing concern for him, as he felt that the defence was seeking a general trawl of highly sensitive files. Judge Carroll directed that the relevant files should be put at the disposal of Mr Charlton for perusal as to whether they were relevant and should be disclosed.

This was to cause some unease for Mr McDonagh SC, who informed the judge that his clients, the attorney general, Michael McDoughal, and the garda commissioner, had been in consultation and, if necessary, would appeal the order to the Supreme Court. A stay was put on the order.

Eventually, an accommodation was reached: a senior official from the DPP's office would examine the files and report the findings to Mr Charlton. If necessary, Judge Carroll would also read them.

This should have been the end of the matter, but it was not. It was revealed that Catherine Nevin's legal team had enquired whether an agreement had been entered into during the investigation between the Gardaí, the attorney general or the DPP, and any or all of the main witnesses: Heapes, Jones and McClean. I emphatically replied to the Chief State Solicitor's

Office: 'There was no agreement entered into.'

The Special Branch files were finally handed to the judge; she ruled that privilege would be continued in relation to the documents. She further stated: 'There is absolutely nothing to suggest that Tom Nevin was a member of the IRA or held any sympathy with, or for, their views.'

The jury was unaware of all this, as they remained in the jury room throughout the legal arguments. It was at last time to get the show on the road, but things would be short-lived. On 26 January, the trial was prematurely brought to a halt – and this after more than fifty witnesses had been dealt with. After breaking for lunch, the court was due to resume at 2.15 PM, but all was not right. The defence and prosecution teams were not present, and access to the balcony area of the courtroom was refused. At 3.30 PM, the court resumed, and Judge Carroll dismissed the jury. It transpired that someone had heard the jury's discussions in the jury room. This was brought to the notice of Judge Carroll, who took the only course open to her and dismissed the jury.

On 7 February, a second jury was sworn in, but it was also dismissed the following day. One of the jurors was pregnant and sitting through a long trial would be too demanding, both physically and mentally, for her. Finally, on 14 February 2000, a third jury was sworn in. Six men and six women would make up the jury, and on their shoulders would rest the responsibility for deciding Catherine Nevin's guilt or innocence.

Peter Charlton, in his opening address to the jury, advised them to 'listen carefully to the evidence, examine it, and decide for or against it'. He asked them to have an open mind and to use common sense. He explained fully, in layman's language, the meaning of murder and soliciting murder. To be guilty of murder, it is not necessary to pull the trigger. Soliciting was only a crime on the part of the person doing it. If the person asked does not consent, then it is no crime on his or her part, but if there is consent, then the crime becomes a 'conspiracy'.

He said that the prosecution would show that Tom Nevin was murdered at the behest of his wife, and the scene so arranged to give the impression that a robbery had gone wrong. But until such time as this was proven, it would remain only a theory. Mrs Nevin stood before them, presumed innocent.

Breaking the ice and being the first witness called was one James Curry, the operator at Bell Communications alarm monitoring company. He gave evidence of receiving an alert alarm notification from Jack White's Inn at 4.31 AM on 19 March 1996. He phoned Wexford Garda Station, and the information was in turn passed to Garda Paul Cummiskey at Arklow Garda Station.

Garda Cummiskey took the stand. He and Garda McAndrew responded to the call and were the first Gardaí to arrive at the scene. The journey took approximately ten minutes.

He testified that he knew the premises well; he lived just a few miles from it. He noticed that the front hall door was slightly open, by about six inches. As he approached the door, he could hear the moans of a woman, and on entering the hall saw Catherine. Her wrists were tied and there was a gag in her mouth, which was quite loose and was easily removed. He looked for signs of a forced entry or intruders, but found neither. In the kitchen he saw Tom Nevin lying on his back, obviously dead. He was lying in a pool of blood, with a gaping hole on the right hand side of his chest. Tom's glasses were in the reading position and he had a pen in his right hand. His wallet was sitting outside the right inside pocket of his coat. Commiskey was familiar with guns but got no smell of gunpowder. Dr N. Buggle, of Arklow, arrived and pronounced Tom Nevin dead.

Catherine, he noted, was wearing only a purple-coloured silk nightshirt, and white panties. When asked what had happened, she replied: 'He came into the bedroom, he had a knife and a hood over his head.' Garda McAndrew undid without any difficulty a blue dressing gown belt tied around her wrists. More difficult to release were cloth headbands, also tied around her wrists. Other than red marks on her wrists, he didn't notice any other marks. There was a nylon stocking loosely hanging around her neck, which had been holding a black pair of panties in her mouth as a gag.

Catherine kept repeating: 'Where's Tom, where's Tom?' He went to Catherine's bedroom and noticed that the main ceiling light was on. The phone on the bedside locker furthest from the entrance door was off the hook, and the receiver was on the ground. The bedroom was untidy, with clothes and boxes scattered about. There was a glass half filled with what he thought was spirits.

A portable TV was lying on the ground, on the landing, against the banister of the stairs. There was a trail of jewellery down the stairs, and on into the hallway and the lounge. An upturned jewellery box was also in the lounge, lying on the floor.

The family's Opel Omega car was missing, presumed stolen by the intruders. He described the weather that night as very bad, windy and raining.

Crime correspondents put garda witnesses into two groupings: those who can easily be broken, and those who cannot, even under the fiercest cross-examination. An eminent crime correspondent was heard to whisper to a nearby detective: 'Mr McEntee won't get any joy from him.'

McEntee was on his feet to test the mettle of the first garda witness. 'The Arklow Gardaí in general don't like Mrs Nevin, do they?' Cummiskey disagreed: 'The Gardaí had no difficulty with either Mr or Mrs Nevin.'

'Are you not aware,' McEntee enquired, 'that a young employee at Jack White's pub, a fifteen-year-old girl, had made allegations against a garda from Arklow in July 1991. Is it not true that two members of the Gardaí had given her a lift in the patrol car, late at night or in the early morning? One of them was dropped off, leaving the girl and the remaining garda alone in the car. He then made a sexual advance to her. Mrs Nevin and her husband, on hearing of the girl's ordeal, made statements to the garda authorities about the alleged assault.'

Mr McEntee's cross-examination continued. 'Is it not true that prior to your testimony, you said the door was slightly ajar, now you say it was ajar by about six inches?' 'Six inches to me is slightly ajar,' Garda Cummiskey replied.

As this line of cross-examination was introduced by Mr McEntee, I concluded that the existence of bad blood between the two parties would be used to try to blacken the conduct of Arklow-based Gardaí over the years towards the Nevins. Should Mr McEntee succeed in his efforts to show them as having a vendetta against the Nevins because Catherine had exercised her lawful and constitutional right to speak out about criminal activity against two of them, this would show them as dishonest and corrupt. This line of attack by McEntee would continue throughout the trial.

Detective Pat Mulcahy and Sergeant Brian Duffy were to have much contact with Gerry Heapes, with whom they seemed to hit it off. Mulcahy was giving evidence about meeting Heapes and his wife Breda at their home on 31 July 1996. Heapes joined them in their car and gave them directions. When passing the Grasshopper pub, Heapes told them to stop the car and stated: 'That's the pub.' From there, he directed them to Blanchardstown and, pointing at one of the banks, said: 'I will tell you about it later.' From there he directed them to Phoenix Park, through Islandbridge, over the bridge and along South Circular Road towards the Rialto entrance to St James's Hospital. He then directed them to a street off South Circular Road, and pointed to a house on the right hand side of it. The Gardaí were aware that this was one of Catherine's houses.

He made a statement to them outlining the meetings he had had with Catherine, and her plans to have her husband killed. He declined to sign the statement, as he wished to consult his people before doing so. He never signed the statement.

On 3 August, they were again on the road, and being directed once more by Heapes. This time, Gerry directed them to a road in the Phoenix Park, which led down by the Wellington Monument, and asked them to stop the car there. In that area, and at a location pointed out by Gerry, one had a clear view of the bridge at Islandbridge. This was the spot pointed out to him by Catherine, from where Tom could be seen driving his car from the flats at Mayfield Road to the bank at Blanchardstown.

These routes, as pointed out by Catherine to him, were the same in every detail as the routes taken by Tom and as verified by the employee, Billy Randle, who invariably accompanied Tom from Jack White's pub to Dublin each Monday (or Tuesday after a bank holiday weekend).

Detective Garda Joe Collins's evidence would prove to be highly significant; he was one of only two Gardaí, the other being Detective Sergeant Fergus O'Brien, whom Catherine would deal with. When he arrived at the pub on the morning of the murder, he saw Catherine sitting on a couch in the sitting room and tried to put her at ease. There were some reddish marks on her wrists, which had been tied. Other than those, he saw no further evidence of any marks or abrasions. She outlined the following details to him: 'She went to bed about 12.30 AM. Dominic McElligot left at about 12 midnight. One man with a knife, looking for jewellery. Someone shouted and I heard a noise like a falling saucepan. There was another fellow throwing things around.

'He tied my hands and put something on my feet and mouth. Got my feet free and came downstairs and pressed the panic button. Tom did the lodgement; the amount is in the books. Is the money taken? I don't know if he took all the jewellery. Is he [Tom] really dead? Told me he was going to kill me, I didn't see anybody except the fellow who tied me up.

'The front door was open when I came downstairs. I tried to catch my nails in it, to open it, but I couldn't. It wasn't fully open, just barely. None of the staff stay here on a Monday night, of a bank holiday weekend. The man in my bedroom had a knife; he held my head down on the pillow. I don't know how they got in. Tom made up the lodgement.

'The lights were off. I got the legs free. I tried to dial 999. I left Dominic out. Tom always has a wallet which never has less than £500 in it. Never looked for money, about £400 in my handbag.'

Later that same day, accompanied by Detective Sergeant O'Brien, he interviewed Catherine again with a view to getting her account of events in written form. She replied: 'Joe, I gave you a statement earlier today.' He informed her that what he had taken were notes and he now needed a written statement. Her reply was: 'I will make no statement or sign anything. I want a guarantee from a superior officer – and not Superintendent Flynn, I don't trust him – that my statement won't end up on the desk in Arklow, to have it doctored like the other statements. I don't trust anybody in Arklow, present company excluded.'

He showed her the jewellery box which had been found in the lounge, and the items of jewellery scattered around the premises. It was all there, she said, but maybe two sovereign rings were missing. She later said that they were not stolen. In fact, not a single item of jewellery had been stolen.

After the funeral of Tom Nevin, Detective Sergeant O'Brien and Detective Collins went to the pub. Catherine told them: 'After letting Sergeant McElligot out the night of the murder, she closed the hall door, pushed it closed, it Yale-locked, and she mortise-locked it by turning the Chubb key.' Earlier, she had told them: 'Sergeant McElligot pulled the door after him and it Yale-locked.'

On 23 March 1996, she told them, the amount of money stolen was £16,500, made up of £4,500 payment they received from displaying billboards, £1,800 of her own personal cash, £2,000 in sterling, £3,000 takings for 11 to 14 March, £500 takings for Friday 15 March, £1,700 for 16 March and £1,500 for 18 March 1996.

He also outlined how he was present on 4 April 1996 when firearm tests were carried out on the premises. The shots were discharged in the kitchen where Tom Nevin had been murdered. He took up position about ten yards from the entrance to the pub. From there, he could clearly hear the shots being discharged, and could say that they were exactly that: i.e. gunshots. For the sixth shot, he was positioned in the bedroom next to Catherine's, and likened this shot to a loud thud. There was no odour in the bedroom after this shot had been discharged.

On 12 April, both he and Detective Sergeant O'Brien were in the sitting room at the pub talking to Catherine. She absented herself for a few minutes and he saw an opened address/telephone book. The name 'Gerry Heapes' and a phone number were written on the opened page, and he made a note of it. After the search of the pub on 18 May 1996, he again saw this book but the name and phone number were scribbled over on the front and reverse side of the page.

On 29 April, he asked Catherine if she knew a person called John Ferguson. She denied knowing or having had any contact with such a person, either in person or by phone.

On 4 May, Catherine informed him and Fergus O'Brien that Tom had died without making a will. She had also been in contact with a 'tea leaf' (slang for a thief or criminal), at Dolphins Barn, Dublin, and let it be known that she was offering a substantial reward for information leading to the conviction of the people responsible for Tom's murder. In this interview, she also told them: 'You'll find nothing on the phone, Tom Kennedy told me not to use it, as it could be tapped.'

Their last interview with her was on 4 December 1996, and as usual it was held at Jack White's pub. She was sitting with Tom Kennedy in the lounge as they entered. Joe told her that there were a few questions they wished to ask her. Without hesitating, she replied: 'Joe, I told you before I have no problem answering questions through my solicitor.' Certain allegations had been made against her, he informed her. She replied: 'If you want to talk to me, it will be in the presence of my solicitor.' He then told her that two men had alleged that she had solicited them to murder her husband, and immediately gave her the legal caution. She stood up from the stool, walked to the bar, got a piece of paper and wrote on it 'Garrett Sheehan' and his phone number, and handed the piece of paper to him. He then said to her: 'I take it you don't want to answer these allegations?' She replied: 'Yes, thanks very much, get in touch with my solicitor.'

During her period of detention at Enniscorthy Garda Station, he was one of the many Gardaí who interviewed her. She had refused to answer any of the questions put to her, or to sign the notes taken of them.

Detective Collins's approach to cross-examination is so relaxed that one could be forgiven for holding the view that his attitude borders on indifference. Nothing could be further from the truth: if a question can be answered by a simple yes or no, then that is the option invariably taken by him. One eminent barrister's description of him in cross-examination is most apt: 'Getting information out of him in cross-examination is as painful as having teeth extracted.' Would Paddy McEntee SC succeed where all of his contempories had failed?

Collins's evidence was gone through in detail by Mr McEntee, especially the entries in Catherine's address/telephone book. Paddy suggested that these had been erased when Tom found out that Heapes had phoned looking for an apartment to rent. Tom was annoyed and, as a result, the entries were there and then erased. Joe replied: 'The entries were definitely in the book on 12 April 1996.' This was later confirmed by Detective Sergeant O'Brien when giving his evidence.

The issue of bad blood was raised once more by Mr McEntee. 'This was a figment of Catherine's imagination. Mrs Nevin had acknowledged in the *Irish Independent*, issue of 18 April 1996, her gratitude, and thanks to An Garda Síochána, especially to Assistant Commissioner McHugh, Detective Sergeant O'Brien and Detective Joe Collins,' Collins politely answered. Mr McEntee seemed to accept that nothing was to be gained from his efforts with Detective Collins.

Detective Sergeant Fergus O'Brien, Wicklow Garda Station, made his way to the witness box. If facial expressions meant anything, here was a man who was completely at ease with the task confronting him as he took his seat in the witness box.

He had made copious notes of the interviews, which were many and varied, with Catherine, and on occasions during his evidence made reference to them. He recounted some which were of relevance in giving an insight into the workings of this incredible woman.

On one occasion, she contacted him concerning a satellite dish which, she alleged, had been stolen from the roof of the pub. On examining the brackets, he noticed that they were rusty – giving a clear indication that there had been no dish on the roof in a long time. The staff confirmed that the dish had been missing for a considerable length of time.

On 26 April 1996, she reported the loss/larceny of her driving licence and passport, and also of Tom's. They had been in a safe, which also contained the papers annulling Tom's previous marriage. Her driving licence was later found on the premises; again, there was no evidence that anything had been stolen.

On 29 April, she reported the larceny of £2,000 from a cash box in the storeroom. She blamed staff for giving information about the location of the box, and about its contents, to the raiders. On 5 May, Catherine also told O'Brien that she had hired a private detective, but he had not come up with anything useful.

His evidence, like the part he played in the investigation, was excellent, and as expected there were no hiccups during cross-examination.

Assistant Commissioner Jim McHugh, who was then in charge of the South Eastern Region, which covers Arklow Garda Station, was called. He had thirty-eight years' service in An Garda Síochána, including twenty-five years' involvement in crime investigation and intelligence gathering.

He arrived at the scene around 9 AM and noted the position of the body of Tom Nevin on the kitchen floor. He saw a biro between the fingers of his right hand, and Tom's spectacles, which were in the reading position. A half-pint glass, which contained a small amount of what appeared to be stout, rested on the worktop. A wallet was lying on the inside of the right-hand side of Tom's jacket. A four-legged tubular stool lay on the floor on the left side of the deceased. He saw cheques and other documents on a worktop. In the lounge, there was a large quantity of items of jewellery on the floor, and also an upturned wooden jewellery box. There were also items of jewellery on the stairs leading to the bedrooms.

He noticed that the ceiling light in Catherine's bedroom was on, and the curtains were drawn. There was a newspaper on the bed. There were two bedside lockers, one on either side of the bed; a phone on the far bedside locker was off the hook, and the receiver was lying on the floor. The bedroom was in a general state of disorder.

Three of the five drawers in the chest of drawers had been removed. There were two cardboard boxes and a suitcase on the floor. A number of items remained in a standing position on both bedside lockers. A portable TV lay on its screen in the corridor, close to the bedroom. He felt it was unusual that armed raiders had contemplated stealing such a cumbersome and relatively inexpensive item. There was no obvious evidence of a systematic search of the bedroom or its contents having taken place.

In the sitting room, he had introduced himself to Catherine and offered his condolences. She gave the impression of being shocked and traumatised. She outlined the sequence of events of that night to him: 'Tom had left two customers home at closing time and he returned at about 12.25 AM. She and (Sergeant) McElligott were the only persons then on the premises. She walked Dominic to the front hall door, he left, and she closed the door behind him. She then told Tom she was going to bed. He was tidying up in the bar.'

She read for a short while and fell asleep, but was awakened by a masked man pushing her head into a pillow. He had a knife, and kept repeating: 'Where's the fucking jewellery? I'll fucking kill you.' She was conscious of a second person being in the room but didn't see him. Her hands were tied behind her back, and her feet drawn up in a backwards movement towards her hands. He then stuffed something into her mouth and tied something around her mouth, knotting it at the back of her head. When all this was happening, she heard a noise downstairs like a saucepan falling on the floor.

After what seemed like ages, she eventually undid the knots which bound her hands and feet together. She tried to dial 999 but, as her hands were still tied behind her back, the receiver fell to the floor. Having made her way to the front door, she noticed that it was slightly open, and tried to open it fully to get on to the roadway, stop a motorist, and raise the alarm. She failed in her attempt, and then pressed the panic button in the hall inside the front door. She remained there until the Gardaí arrived.

The assistant commissioner outlined how he had asked her: 'Did you not, during your horrific ordeal, think to look for your husband or call out his name?' She told him 'that for whatever reason, it never crossed her mind. It was only when Gardaí McAndrew and Cummiskey arrived, and she asked where is Tom, that it entered her mind.' She couldn't describe her attacker.

On 28 March, Catherine phoned the assistant commissioner and he went to the pub. She claimed that Tom was an alcoholic and could be violent. He had assaulted her on more than one occasion and she was hospitalised once as a result of a beating by him, she said. About seven years previously, they had contemplated separating but had decided against it. Tom had said: 'Who would have either of us at that stage of our lives?' She didn't believe Tom was involved in any relationship, and while she had male friends, she wasn't intimately involved with them.

His next visit to the pub was on 3 April, when he was accompanied by Detective Tom Byrne. Catherine gave permission for firearm tests to be carried out at the premises. She kept her bedroom locked and would not under any circumstances allow Gardaí in it during the tests.

During the trial, Catherine's attentiveness was seen to fluctuate, depending on which witness was giving evidence. During McHugh's evidence, it was noticeable that she was taking in every syllable he uttered. She had sought him out during the investigation, as he was the one highest up the pecking order.

Detective Garda Jim McCawl was next into the witness box. Based at Arklow Garda Station for most of his career, he was the Gorey district representative on the Garda Representative Association for many years. It was in this capacity that he was indirectly involved with Catherine, as a result of her many complaints against Gardaí based in Arklow. Catherine hated the ground he walked upon, and she was certainly never included on his Christmas card list.

Like all individuals, Jim has faults, one of the biggest being that, when he was cross-examined in court, he was apt to lose his cool. He and Paddy McEntee SC had crossed swords previously, and each was fully conversant with the other's abilities. McEntee would also try to turn Jim's dislike for Catherine to his advantage. However, the fire and brimstone expected in cross-examination never materialised, because Jim's answers were brief and very much to the point. He was coolness personified.

Detective Garda William Brennan entered the witness box to give his evidence. He is a member of the Ballistics section, with eighteen years' experience in the examination and testing of firearms and ammunition and the examination of scenes of serious crimes. Describing the premises, he noted that the only external door that was not locked was the front entrance hall door. Most of the windows, and the rearmost doors, had not been opened in some time, were stiff, and bore deposits of cobwebs.

The building was protected by a burglar alarm system, with four external alarm boxes, and in addition there was a panic-attack alarm linked directly to a twenty-four-hour monitoring station in Dublin. This panic alarm could be triggered by pressing any one of five push buttons and two panic-attack buttons located throughout the premises. One of the fixed panic buttons was located on the frame of the front door to the left side behind a curtain, at a height of 4 foot 6 inches above floor level. This button, which had no reset key fitted, had been pressed. The alarm was functioning properly, as were all the triggering devices. There was no evidence of a forced entry.

In the kitchen, he examined Tom Nevin's body and the surrounding area. There were what appeared to be portions of fibre shotgun wads and white polystyrene granules on the outer surface of the jacket and jumper. There was a black leather wallet lying on the top of the right inside pocket of the jacket; the pocket was badly torn, so that the pocket lining had become detached. The wallet was not removed or the pocket torn due to the shot being discharged into the jacket, as the hole was not in line with the pocket. The contents of the wallet seemed to be intact.

He took measurements of the hole in the deceased man's shirt, and this corresponded with the large gunshot entry wound on the deceased's chest area, below his right nipple. There were four large-gauge lead pellets lodged in the deceased man's left chest area. These had entered through his right chest, passed through his heart, causing massive injury, and continued into the left armpit area in a slight upwards trajectory.

In the liquor store beside the kitchen, there was an opened floor safe, which was empty. There was a single-barrel shotgun lying on a shelf. He located a small, covert wall safe concealed over the top shelf in this store; this contained two antique cluster rings and a gold bracelet.

He noted that there was no sign of any ransacking or disturbance in any of the ground-floor rooms, including the bar and lounge area. The cash tills were all open and the cash floats, of about £80 in notes and coin in each till, were untouched.

On the second floor were two bedrooms and a small bathroom. Despite the untidy appearance of these rooms, they had not been ransacked or disturbed.

Mrs Nevin's bedroom is a large double bedroom in which the door opened inwards. The main centre light was on. There was a huge amount of prescription drugs both on top of and inside the lockers beside her bed. Also beside one of the lockers was a black ladies' handbag, and the contents were spread out on the ground beside it. These included a bank deposit book, a brown purse, bank cards, a few coins and other assorted documents.

Inside the locker was a remote controller panic attack button unit. On the windowsill behind the bed, he saw and examined a second unit. These were in working order, could have been used, but had not been.

The shotgun found in the store and registered in Catherine's name did not appear to have been discharged recently, and was definitely not used in Tom Nevin's murder.

Mr McEntee went through the motions of cross-examination, but Detective Brennan's evidence had been precise, accurate and flawless. It was noticeable that the jury were fascinated by the significance of his evidence, as they were making copious notes during his spell in the witness box. They must have wondered why Catherine had not activated any of the panic attack button systems, one of which was on the windowsill beside her bed.

Detective Garda John O'Neill, Fingerprint Section, Garda Headquarters, examined the scene on 20 March. He found no evidence of a forced entry. He saw Catherine Nevin with a blood-stained pocket from the deceased's jacket, which he took possession of.

The jewellery box he saw on the floor in the lounge was examined, and prints taken from it were those of Catherine Nevin. No other prints or marks were found on it. O'Neill saw boxes used for storing goods in her bedroom, which had been thrown out of the press rather than removed and systematically searched. The three drawers which had been removed from the chest of five had prints lifted from them which indicated that the owner of them had been wearing surgical or fine leather gloves. No other room was in a disturbed state.

Detective Garda Thomas Carey, Ballistics Section, gave evidence of seeing a safe containing bundles of money totalling £4,000. This safe was locked but had been opened by the Gardaí. On one of the shelves he found a portable safe box containing two gold rings and a bracelet. This was in a store to the right of the kitchen. He noticed a cash float in a wooden lock-up press which amounted to several hundred pounds in various coinage. Sunken into the floor was a floor safe, which was empty; it was open, and the lid of it, with the key inserted, was on the floor beside the safe.

The front hall door was fitted with a Yale door latch and a mortise lock, none of which were damaged. There was no forced entry via this door, or elsewhere.

Dr Mary Casey, a forensic scientist at the Department of Justice, stated that when she carried out an analysis on the blood and urine samples of Tom Nevin, she found that the blood contained an alcohol level that would be just above the drink-driving limit. These results would cast serious doubts on Catherine's earlier statements that Tom was an alcoholic who drank about one litre of whiskey per day.

Dr John Harbison was the state pathologist, and was professor of forensic medicine at the Royal College of Surgeons and also lecturer in medical jurisprudence at Trinity College Dublin. He was regarded by his peers as the best in his field. He was instantly recognisable as he made his way to the witness box; he gave a slight nod of the head towards the judge and counsels for the state and defence. All would have crossed swords previously.

Professor Harbison arrived at the pub at about 12.45 PM on the morning of the murder, and carried out his usual tests at the scene. Tom Nevin's body was lying on the flat of his back in the kitchen, fully clothed, with his jacket open. Blood was visible beside the right side of the deceased's abdomen and a little beside his right shoulder.

The room temperature was 19 degrees centigrade, at 1.50 PM. There was an entry wound from a shotgun. There was no satelliting (independent pellet marking around the margin of the wound). This suggested a range of not more than a yard, although perhaps two yards would be the outer limit. A shotgun seemed the certain cause of the wound.

At the post mortem examination, x-rays of the chest, left shoulder, and left neck regions showed four opacities, consistent with large pellets in the soft tissues, in, around and below the left shoulder joint. There were four exit wounds on the left side of the back. Other injuries included abrasions on the left lower shin, and there was bruising associated with the abrasions. These would have been caused by some object striking the leg in an upwards and backwards direction, or the deceased's leg falling in a downwards and forwards direction against a fixed object.

Professor Harbison's summary and conclusions were: 'The deceased, Thomas Nevin, in my opinion died of acute cerebral anoxia, as a result of instant stoppage of his circulation as a result of massive gunshot injuries to his heart, aorta and pulmonary trunk. The deceased had been hit by a single discharge of a shotgun into the right side of his chest, from the right front to the left back. I agreed with Detective William Brennan that this was consistent with 12 bore ammunition of lg size. The range of the shot, while necessitating verification by test-card finding, was certainly not more than two yards and could have been less.

'The brain may remain alive for four minutes or so, without circulation, but it is unlikely consciousness would last for more than thirty seconds. Theoretically, he could have moved after being shot and even remain standing until he lost consciousness. Neither the pools of blood beside the body or slight stains a distance from it suggest to me signs of a struggle. This is further suggested by the glasses on his nose and the biro in his hand. He appears to have been surprised while counting the money.'

Jane Murphy, a small, frail, elderly woman who lives quite near the pub, had been employed there for ten years prior to the murder. She was very well known locally and considered to be a bit of a character. I was talking to her the morning she was to give her evidence. 'No,' she told me, 'I'm not a bit nervous, sure all I can do is tell the truth, and I will tell everything I know.' Somehow I felt that the occasion, especially when she was seated in the witness box, would get to her, and so it proved.

She was led very tenderly, and with great expertise, by the prosecution in her direct evidence, but she was very nervous. She had never been inside a court previously and now, aged in excess of seventy years, she was being called upon to give evidence against her employer of ten years, who stood charged with the murder of her husband. Her voice was barely audible, even though she was asked on a number of occasions if she could speak a little louder.

Eventually, and after much effort, she told the court that she remembered a Mr Ferguson (Pat Russell) making phone calls to the premises. Did he ever stay at or visit the pub? 'Not that I know,' she replied. 'Yeah, and the judge from Arklow made phone calls.' Did he ever come to the pub and stay? 'Yeah, he did,' came the reply.

Caroline Strahan was just a few months short of twenty-one years when the murder happened. She had been employed there on two separate occasions, first in 1991 and then in 1992. Her duties combined waitressing and cleaning: twelve-hour working days were the norm. She didn't get on well with Mrs Nevin, who often shouted at her. She knew that Tom and Catherine didn't get on well and slept in separate bedrooms. There were constant rows and arguments.

Tom Kennedy used to visit a lot. Caroline Strahan saw him in bed with Catherine; they were under the covers, and Tom

Kennedy had nothing on top. Catherine had a relationship with him. Mr McEntee interrupted this evidence, saying that his evidence was contradicting hers. 'That's what it seemed like to me,' came the girl's reply. She knew that Catherine was friendly with the judge from Arklow.

The jury was hearing for the first time particulars of Catherine's affections for Tom Kennedy. Caroline had in fact, in a second statement made to the Gardaí, stated that she had seen Kennedy and Catherine together in bed on numerous occasions. Catherine would ring from her bedroom and she would bring up breakfast to them. This was not given in evidence.

Eileen Byrne worked at the pub for six months in 1993, but left because she didn't like Catherine. She remembers reporting for work one morning at 8 AM and seeing four or five Gardaí drinking in the pub. Tom Kennedy's retirement party had taken place there the previous night. Tom Nevin was behind the bar, had had a good few drinks, and seemed agitated. He said to her aloud: 'This will all end in tears.' She never saw Tom Nevin talk to either the judge or Kennedy. There were lots of arguments between Catherine and Tom Nevin.

Orla Glennon, a niece of Tom Nevin, gave evidence of working at the pub in 1989, in the kitchen and as a waitress. The staff always went to the disco in Arklow on Sunday or Monday nights on a bank holiday weekend. After the disco finished, they would come back and stay overnight. Tom and Catherine shared the same bedroom then. She treated Tom very badly, and would berate and belittle him in front of the staff and customers.

Bernie Fleming had been employed at the pub for a year prior to the murder. She had her own set of keys and would let herself in each morning. There was, she stated, a spare set of keys hanging on the rack on the left hand side of the hallway. Six or seven weeks prior to the murder, these keys went missing. Catherine told her that Judge Donnacha O'Buachalla had them, but not to tell Tom Nevin. A day or two later, they were back on the key rack.

She recalled a man giving the name John Ferguson phoning the pub on several occasions prior to the murder. Catherine had issued firm instructions that someone was to come and get her, regardless of the time or where she was, when he called.

The evening prior to the murder, and after finishing work, she was talking to Catherine, who told her she was going to check on the washing machine. Catherine came back about twenty minutes later, and said there was about fifteen minutes remaining on the wash. She and Liz Hudson, some minutes later, went to this same room to put on another wash, but found the machine empty. In fact, it had not been used at all and she knew that Catherine did-n't even know how to use it.

At 9.50 PM that night, she noticed the curtains in the restaurant pulled. She found this very strange, as she had never seen them pulled previously. Catherine seemed on edge all that night. Bernie's attention was also caught by the amount of jewellery that Catherine was wearing: rings on all her fingers, four or five chains, and a thick gold necklace with emeralds set in it around her neck.

Liz Hudson was another employee at Jack White's; she started work there in 1991. She reported for work as usual on 18 March 1996. When Liz was giving evidence, and came to the issue of Catherine having affairs, there was legal argument, and the jury, not for the first time in the trial, were sent to their room.

'I do not wish to raise the issue of discharging the jury,' said Mr McEntee, 'but if this continues I will have to.' Peter Charlton, countering, replied that the next-of-kin issue from her hospital admission in 1991 would be entered in due course to prove Catherine's relationship with Tom Kennedy. (On a hospital admission form in 1991, she had given Tom Kennedy as next of kin.) He realised the dangers inherent in this, but felt that he had no choice because of the defence challenge to the evidence so far before the jury. Judge Carroll ruled in Mr McEntee's favour, and the evidence relating to next of kin was not allowed.

Liz Hudson confirmed that she was speaking from her own

personal knowledge, and her evidence was allowed to continue. Mr McEntee was incensed at the judge's ruling.

The jury was again in place, and the issue of keys for the premises was raised. Catherine had asked Liz for a loan of her keys to the premises. 'Do you know why?' asked Mr Charlton. 'Because the judge had them,' she was told by Catherine. The keys in question had mysteriously gone missing six or seven weeks before the murder; previously, they had always hung on a key rack in the hall. Just as mysteriously as they had vanished, they reappeared a couple of days later, after her conversation with Catherine.

Alan McGraynor worked as a chef at the pub in 1990. He and Tom went on holidays together twice. It emerged during the trial that Catherine had alleged to Donacha Long, a carpet fitter, that Tom and the barman were having a sexual affair. McGraynor also did bar work. He denied the allegation, as did members of the Nevin family, that Tom was gay. Tom's first wife, June O'Flanagan, also dismissed the suggestion as ludicrous.

Theresa Nevin was married to Sean, a brother of Tom Nevin. She travelled with other members of the Nevin family to the funeral on 21 March 1996. Having entered the pub on their arrival, she was somewhat surprised by what was to greet her. Catherine was having her hair done; on seeing the Nevins, she jumped up, and started to hug Rose, the wife of Noel, another brother of Tom's. Catherine tried to cry, but no tears came.

Catherine started to tell them what had happened. 'The door burst open and two men burst in. She didn't see them as they were wearing balaclavas and one of them had a knife. One of them was shouting: "Get the fucking jewellery."'

Later that evening, back at the pub after the funeral, she was in the kitchen with Catherine, who was talking to her bank manager. She was telling him that she had been in bed reading, when the door was flung open. She told this man that she couldn't see the raiders as it was dark. Rose Nevin, who was also present, picked her up on this and asked: 'But how could you be reading,

Catherine, when it was dark?' Catherine ignored the question.

The entire Nevin family were shocked at Catherine's complete composure, and were taken aback at the apparent lack of shock or emotion at what must have been a most traumatic and frightening experience. They had their suspicions about her from the beginning, and these were compounded by what they had seen and heard prior to, during and after the funeral.

When a file is submitted to the Director of Public Prosecutions, it contains all the evidence gathered by the investigating Gardaí. The file is studied in detail at the DPP's office, and if a decision is taken to prosecute, then much of what could be described as potentially explosive information, gathered in the course of the investigation, was deemed to be of no relevance to the charges before the court. Many meetings were held prior to commencement of the court hearing between staff at the DPP's office and the Gardaí. All these issues were raised and discussed. At the end of the day, the DPP decides what should and should not be included in the book of evidence.

In the case of Catherine Nevin, not everybody who volunteered and made written statements to the Gardaí was called as a witness. The staff were of huge assistance in giving an unambiguous and factual account of Catherine and Tom Nevin's relationship. They had described her behaviour on the night prior to the murder, and details of her extramarital affairs captivated everyone present at the trial. The garda evidence would also certainly have impressed the jury. With the exception of Heapes, Jones, McClean and Russell, the expected appearance in the witness box of former garda inspector Tom Kennedy and local district judge Donnacha O'Buachalla had aroused the most interest, and for obvious reasons.

Loyalty had always been a key part of Tom Kennedy's make-up, both as an officer in An Garda Síochána and in terms of his day-to-day activities. The staff at Jack White's Inn had given explicit details of his shenanigans with Catherine, and one of them had stated that she had seen them in bed together. Would he contradict their evidence, thereby insinuating that they had committed perjury?

The peculiar habit of grinding his teeth, which had unkindly earned him the nickname 'Choppers', was much more in evidence than usual as he took his seat in the witness box. I watched and listened closely as he took the Bible in his hand and uttered the words of the oath: 'I swear by almighty God to tell the truth, the whole truth and nothing but the truth.'

Even before he was to give his evidence, legal argument took place. Peter Charlton demanded as a matter of honour that the defence call him as a witness, thus providing him with an opportunity for cross-examination. Mr Charlton argued: 'If Mr McEntee wishes Inspector Kennedy to say he and Mrs Nevin were not having an intimate relationship, then I wish to be able to cross-examine him on this point.' Judge Carroll ruled in favour of the defence. Kennedy would therefore be a witness for the prosecution.

Kennedy confirmed that he knew Tom and Catherine Nevin and that he had become very friendly with them over the years. He also knew Judge O'Buachalla, who was a regular visitor at Jack White's. He knew of gossip about Catherine and himself. No, he had never had a sexual relationship with Catherine Nevin. He was over sixty years old, and sex wasn't an issue for him. 'I am not into that, Judge; I am a happily married man. I value my marriage and my family too much.'

Sometimes he visited Mrs Nevin's bedroom when she was present in it; mostly during her bouts of illness and when he was requested to go there. Occasionally, he would get her medication in Wicklow town and take it to her bedroom. When pressed, he said that it was Tom Nevin or staff members who had requested him to see Catherine in her bedroom. Many in the courtroom were amazed at this utterance – that the husband had actually asked him to go to his wife's bedroom. Kennedy said that he never stayed overnight at the Nevins' property at Mountshannon Road, Dublin.

There was no need for cross-examination, though Mr McEntee went through the motions. It was abundantly clear that Kennedy was not going to play the part of Judas. Kennedy may have done no visible damage to himself by his evidence in the witness box, but did he besmear all the good the Garda Síochána stands for? He was also to cast as liars the staff who had given evidence of his affair with Catherine Nevin.

Did he not spare a thought for his long-suffering wife or the fine children he was father to? Mrs Kennedy, in an interview after the trial, declared: 'Catherine Nevin destroyed our marriage.' Yes, Catherine Nevin did destroy the Kennedys' marriage, but Tom Kennedy was an active participant in that destruction. He found the lure of Catherine Nevin irresistible. It wasn't a spur-of-the-moment decision, but when it was made, it was final; Catherine would make sure of that.

27

Judge O'Buachalla

There was huge anticipation of the entrance into the witness box of Judge Donnacha O'Buachalla, due to his friendship with Catherine, and the fact that he was disliked by some Arklow-based Gardaí. His professional relationship with Gardaí Michael Murphy and Vincent Whelan has already been outlined.

The granting by him of a pub licence to Catherine Nevin for Jack White's Inn some time after she had been charged with his murder had also received huge media coverage. O'Buachalla saw nothing irregular in the manner in which he had granted the licence, despite the fact that most of the requirements for such applications were ignored by him. The hearing was not in open court, the requirement to give written notice to the local garda superintendent was ignored, and notice, as required to appear in newspapers, was also ignored. There was no prior written application to the relevant court clerk. It is therefore my view that no application existed, and nothing could be granted. Tom Nevin's dislike for the judge was well known to staff members: Jeanie Murphy had heard him call the judge 'a fucking ole bollocks' during a phone conversation.

Judge O'Buachalla was sitting in familiar surroundings, but on this occasion he was in the witness box at a murder trial in the Central Criminal Court. His every word would be carefully listened to. He walked briskly to the witness box.

Commencing his evidence in a clear, audible voice, he commented on his friendship with Catherine and the late Tom Nevin. He had an excellent relationship with them both, he said. On average, he would visit the pub two or three times a week, sometimes in the morning, but the frequency and times of his visit would be dependent on his other work commitments.

'I never stayed overnight at the pub,' he said, 'and at no stage did I have keys for it, and I didn't see any such set of keys.' He had visited the pub with his wife and family; the last such occasion was the weekend of Tom's murder. They had a meal in the evening; Tom joined them at the table for a few minutes.

Mr McEntee was on his feet to begin his cross-examination: 'It has been suggested that you were involved in some affair.' Mr Charlton rose quickly to reject this statement. 'It has never been suggested, my lord. Perhaps the jury could be asked to retire briefly,' asked Mr Charlton. Judge Carroll agreed.

After some further argument, it was agreed that it should be put to O'Buachalla that it had been implied that he was having an affair.

Once the jury had returned, Mr McEntee continued with his cross-examination. He stated: 'Liz Hudson and Bernie Fleming have given evidence from which it could be implied that you were having some sort of an irregular sexual affair with Mrs Nevin.'

'That is not so, that is not true,' replied O'Buachalla.

'Did anything ever happen that may have given rise to that suggestion?'

'No, nothing that I am aware of,' replied O'Buachalla.

Donnacha O'Buachalla walked briskly from the witness box and left the courtroom. His ordeal was over; or was it?

28

PAT RUSSELL

Pat Russell, alias John Ferguson/Fergus, was in the witness box explaining his association with Catherine, which had to do with her desire to get rid of her present accountants, Coopers & Lybrand. He had been phoning Jack White's Inn regularly for a number of weeks prior to the murder. As we have seen, Catherine had issued prior instructions to staff to get her immediately when he phoned, and also to man the extension (and to make sure nobody else was listening in) when she was speaking to him. His name was not to be mentioned to anyone else.

He said he first met Catherine in the Sinn Féin advice centre in Finglas around 1985. He had been an active member of Sinn Féin but began to dissociate himself from them in the late 1980s. He knew John Jones through Sinn Féin and also from the advice centre. He kept in touch with the Nevins, and called into Jack White's Inn occasionally after Tom and Catherine had taken over ownership of it. He was aware that Catherine was trying to get someone to murder her husband.

Catherine made contact with him by phone and asked if he would take on the financial accounts for her. He wasn't keen on doing this, and in any event wasn't qualified to sign an audit. They had a meeting in the Davenport Hotel, Dublin, in January 1996. She was alone, and told him that Tom was drinking heavily, and wasn't as actively involved in the running of the pub as he should be. She wanted to buy his share of it but knew that Tom would never consent to this. Could he fix her up with new accountants, she enquired.

Russell agreed to try and arrange a meeting between her and a new firm as soon as possible. It was evident that Tom was to be left in the dark about changing accountants, as she issued firm instructions to him about making contact by phone with her at the pub. He should speak only to her, and use the pseudonym 'John Fergus'. Under no circumstances was he to use his real name or speak to anyone other than her.

As a result of their meeting in January, he had been in contact with Noel Murphy, an accountant with Paffrey Murphy chartered accountants in Cork city. He set up meetings between Catherine and Noel Murphy, but she failed to turn up for the first meeting. The rearranged meeting was to be held at his office. She gave a firm commitment to attend and would, she stated, be accompanied by her husband, Tom. At the meeting, Catherine was present but without her husband, whom she stated was still in bed when she had left for Dublin. A lengthy meeting ensued, and Russell understood that there would be a further meeting, at which Tom would be in attendance. On the morning of Tom's murder, Noel Murphy phoned the pub on a number of occasions but got a continuous engaged tone, and was unaware of the happenings there until he heard about it on an RTÉ news bulletin. Murphy then phoned him. So ended his evidence.

The significance of these meetings is obvious, and the jury may have noted Catherine's devious intentions. She wanted to buy Tom out as late as January 1996, but he wouldn't sell. Two months later, he was murdered, and she became the sole owner. Success, it would appear, was Catherine's at last.

29

McClean, Heapes and Jones

To have any chance of proving the charges against Catherine, the evidence of Gerry Heapes, John Jones, William McClean and, to a lesser extent, Pat Russell was crucial.

Initially, with the possible exception of William McClean, all had been reluctant witnesses. Knowing their background, which included criminal records and membership of Sinn Féin, this didn't come as any great surprise. McClean maintained at all times that he was not a member of either the IRA or any loyalist paramilitary group.

It is no secret that the top brass in the republican movement regarded Heapes in the past tense. That may be so, but after making his statements and declining to sign them, he would always give as a reason: 'I'll have to get on to my people first.' He never did in fact sign his statements, but agreed that they were correct.

That Gerry Heapes had been fingered not as a suspect but as a would-be witness by the Gardaí would have been known by the republican movement. Also known by them was the fact that Catherine Nevin had solicited Heapes to murder her husband, or to get his organisation to carry out her wishes. This was a domestic matter between husband and wife, which could have dire consequences for his organisation, should they become involved. The financial rewards, approximately £20,000, would be seen as chicken feed.

William McClean is over-talkative, flamboyant and of a friendly, charismatic disposition. To any barrister acting for an accused person, a witness such as McClean could be likened to manna from heaven. Prosecution counsel would occasionally have some concern or anxiety about a witness freezing under intense cross-examination. With McClean, it was feared that he just would not know when to shut up, thus giving the defence greater scope and latitude to probe every minute detail of his evidence.

I wondered whether he would appreciate the grilling he would face in cross-examination from Mr McEntee. No problem there, he was to counter: 'Sure Paddy and my family go back a long way.' As it transpired, his cross-examination was not by Mr McEntee, but by Mr Paul Burns, McEntee's junior. 'Was he worried about his past being revealed in open court, his previous convictions, his many affairs, including the eighteen-month one he had with Catherine?' I asked him. 'No, not at all, sure anyway that was all years ago.' He strode confidently, even nonchalantly, to the witness box; one hoped that, on conclusion of his evidence, the same gait would be noticeable as he made his exit from it.

Yes, he had three criminal convictions recorded against him. He had first met Catherine Nevin about eleven years ago in the Red Cow pub on the Naas Road in Dublin. Describing her as 'a good-looking bird', he'd 'shifted' her. That was to be the start of an affair which lasted about eighteen months. He knew her as Tom Nevin's wife. The affair was basically sexual. They used Catherine's house in Clondalkin and also the Nevins' flats in Rialto. He had been married in 1969 and separated four years later.

When Catherine and Tom Nevin bought Jack White's Inn, he arranged for their furniture and goods to be moved to the pub. He was there for the official opening and practically every weekend for the next two or three months. He helped out behind the bar when the need arose. The affair continued.

Tom knew about the affair, and even caught Catherine and him in bed together on one occasion. Tom just asked Catherine for some keys and left the room. The matter was never mentioned after this. Eventually, he tired of the affair, and told her that he was putting an end to it, but she was having none of it. He tried this a few times, without success. Sometime later, he devised a plan to end the affair. He brought a girlfriend to the pub, as a way of telling Catherine that the affair was over. She went berserk, as she knew the girl.

In 1990, accompanied by a new girlfriend, he called into Jack White's and met Catherine. He was driving an Opel Kadett, which had the registration number found on the premises in the garda search.

It was noted that the jury was fascinated by his evidence, as they eyed him throughout. Ever the playboy, McClean picked up the glass in front of him and, before filling it with water, enquired: 'Is it clean?'

When Catherine was a patient at St Vincent's Hospital, around 1990, she phoned him, and he called to the hospital the following day. She professed her still-burning love for him and expressed a desire to rekindle the affair. He wasn't interested, and told her so.

Out of the blue – and very much to the point – Catherine asked him to do something for her. 'There is £20,000 for you to get rid of Tom, and we can get back together again.' He listened but had no intention of complying with her request. She also told him: 'Get him when he is going to the bank or the flats. You have the contacts.' He was shocked, and looked at her and said 'No fucking way, Catherine', and left.

Paul Burns BL, for the defence, queried the truthfulness of the affair as suggested by McClean: 'There was no affair. Was he not just a friend of her husband's and helped in the removal of their furniture from Clondalkin to Jack White's?'

McClean replied that not only was there an affair, but he also stayed overnight at the pub after the official opening and on numerous weekends thereafter. He helped out behind the bar occasionally. He would prove he was at the opening, and also that he served behind the bar. 'Ask the customer who drank there with the deformed hand.' This was a reference to Paddy Doyle, a local fisherman. McClean also remembers serving members of the Gardaí with drink on occasions.

Burns was warming to the task. 'Are you wanted in the North to serve a three-month sentence imposed on you at Clogher Magistrates Court in 1973, for deception, a conviction subsequently appealed unsuccessfully?'

'It's a possibility,' replied McClean.

There was some confusion and slight laughter when Burns questioned McClean about his second conviction.

'That was apples,' replied McClean, in his strong Monaghan accent.

'Abbots?' Mr Charlton interjected.

'I bought a load of apples.'

'Well you hardly bought abbots,' mocked Mr Burns.

'I bought a load of apples and exported them to the South, and didn't pay any duty on them. The fella I bought them from came looking for me.'

'Why?' asked Mr Burns.

'Because I didn't pay for them.'

'Is that not a crime?' asked Mr Burns.

'It's only a crime when you're caught,' replied Willie.

When asked whether he had links with paramilitary organisations, McClean replied: 'No, I never had any links with paramilitaries, either loyalist or republican.' He agreed that he had told Catherine he was involved in 'some under-the-counter stuff: wheeling and dealing, a bit of cattle smuggling, spirits as well, that kind of stuff.' Apparently shocked, Mr Burns suggested: 'But that's a crime.'

'It is if you're caught,' came Willie's reply again.

There was much tension when Mr Burns asked McClean: 'Are you not a con man and a deceiver, who would have required para-military protection to smuggle anything across the Monaghan bor-der?' Mr Charlton cautioned that the use of such comments made it exceptionally difficult for people like McClean to come forward as a witness. Mr Burns was later to retract his description of McClean and apologised to the court.

None the worse after his ordeal, Willie swaggered from the witness box, and the Central Criminal Court.

One couldn't help but wonder at the jury's reaction to his evi-dence. He certainly would have come across as a colourful charac-ter. He hadn't tried to hide his past encounters with the law; in fact, he had given explicit details of them. He certainly had the jury's undivided attention, as he had from everybody for the dura-tion of his evidence.

John Jones, the second of the three main witnesses, was about to enter the witness box. He and the well-known republican figure Dessie Ellis had been the proprietors of a TV repair shop, known as Channel Vision Ltd. A Sinn Féin advice centre was also based there. He presented a clean-cut image: he was neatly attired, and sporting a grey beard and grey hair, as he made his way to the witness box.

Commencing his evidence, he recalled meeting Catherine Nevin for the first time in 1984 or 1985, he wasn't sure which. She had walked into the Sinn Féin advice centre, introduced herself and got straight to the purpose of her visit. She wanted to buy a pub. This request from a first-time visitor to the centre seemed most unusual, and was quickly rebuffed by him.

He met her on numerous occasions after this, and learnt that she and her husband, Tom, had secured the lease on the Barry House pub, in Finglas. Her visits to the advice centre intensified. Catherine made the pub available to them to run functions and allowed the sale of *An Phoblacht* on the premises. He was dubious about her and didn't really trust her.

Sometime in 1989, Catherine called to the advice centre and, after some small talk, informed him that she had a proposition for him and his organisation, which could benefit both of them financially. 'She wanted us, Sinn Féin, to stage a robbery in the course of which Tom would be killed. It would be arranged for the Tuesday following the St Patrick's Bank Holiday weekend. The hit would take place when Tom was en route to the bank. He would have the weekend takings, about £25,000, with him.' He told her that his organisation was 'not into that kind of thing' and dismissed the proposition out of hand.

She put the same proposition to him on at least five or six occasions in 1989 and 1990 – until, eventually, he told her she was never again to raise the subject. That was the last occasion he saw her.

Continuing his evidence, he recalled her visiting the advice centre in 1989 or 1990 sporting a pair of black eyes as a result of a beating she alleged Tom had given her.

This ended the direct evidence of another very important witness for the Sate, but his time in the box was far from over. His grilling was undoubtedly the most intense of the three, though he didn't show it, either in his facial expressions or in the quality of his answers. It was essential for the success of the defence's case that Mr McEntee should have some success in casting serious doubts on the testimony of the three main state witnesses, Heapes, Jones and McClean. Should he succeed even with one, then doubt would certainly flow through the minds of the jury, and Mr McEntee would be well on the way to another notable success in his long and illustrious career.

'Who,' asked Mr McEntee, 'did you discuss Mrs Nevin's alleged proposition with – that is, within your organisation?'

'One was Pat Russell, a very well-educated man and with a university education,' Jones replied.

'Who was the other? Did you say there were two? Name the other?' urged Mr McEntee.

'I do not remember,' came the reply. He would not budge on this stance despite serious cross-examination by Mr McEntee.

'Why did you not put a stop to Catherine's solicitations on the very first occasion she put this proposition to you? Why didn't you run her from your office and tell her never to come back, and why did you not warn her husband, either by a personal call or even a phone call, of his wife's murderous intention?'

Jones replied: 'I told her every time she brought up the subject I wanted nothing whatever to do with it, and eventually told her she was never to mention the subject again. I did tell Pat Russell that I had intended going to the Gardaí on hearing of Tom's murder but was advised by him not to, as we both felt they would be visiting us in any event.'

'Catherine Nevin never asked you to murder or get your organisation to murder Tom Nevin, isn't that a fact?'

'You can say what you like, but she did, not once, but on several occasions. Nothing can change that – she did ask me to murder her husband.'

The exchanges were relentless, riveting and exciting. Mr McEntee was at his brilliant best, but despite his best efforts, Jones couldn't be shaken.

'Dessie Ellis,' enquired Mr McEntee. 'Tell us about him.'

'He was a TV repairman, and I believe he was involved with the IRA.' Jones was reluctant to elaborate on what he had already stated about Ellis. Mr McEntee put it to him that he had been questioned about Dessie Ellis after he himself had been arrested in 1981, and also about the making of circuit boards at the TV repair shop. No, came the reply.

Interrupting Jones when he mentioned how he had met Tom Nevin for the first time, Mr McEntee suggested: 'He [Tom Nevin] had republican sympathies.'

'I don't know anything about his sympathies, political or otherwise,' replied Jones.

'Was the *Phoblacht* newspaper not being sold at their pub with Tom's consent?'

'No, it was with Catherine's consent.'

'When were you solicited to do the murder?'

'Sometime in 1989 or 1990.'

In his direct evidence, Jones had stated that he found Catherine's stories and propositions bizarre and unbelievable. Especially so was her tale to him of entering one of her apartments at South Circular Road and being confronted by two SAS men.

Mr McEntee, pouncing on this evidence, suggested: 'Didn't you have use of this flat rent-free for a number of weeks, and isn't it a fact that Catherine had found components in this flat and brought them to you.' The inference here was obvious, concerning the word 'components', referring to bomb parts.

'Not true,' replied Jones.

'As Catherine entered this apartment, two people met her, and one cut her hand with broken glass. She found what seemed like circuit boards there, and told you about this. Didn't you tell her not to tell the Gardaí?'

'That's a lot of rubbish,' replied Jones. 'She told me she was confronted by two SAS men, struggled with them, and they jumped out a window.' I heard a reporter whisper to the person sitting next to him: 'Not making the SAS men like they used to.'

'Did it ever occur to you that you should contact people you know in the IRA about her proposition to you?'

'I do not know anyone in the IRA, and I would not know how to contact them.' He did speak to Pat Russell and another man, whom he couldn't remember. 'Her proposition seemed so unbelievable that it didn't seem worthy of consideration.'

A lighter moment was to follow, after what could be described as heated exchanges between the two: 'Yes, I have a previous conviction. I bought a car but discovered something amiss with the papers. I did not use it; just put it in the garage. But the Special Branch found it and I ended up in court. I got the services of a very eminent barrister, one of the best. I can contest it, or put my trust in the court, my barrister advised me. I chose the second option. You were that barrister, Mr McEntee.'

'That is so, Mr Jones.'

The jury had heard the evidence of two people whom Catherine had propositioned to murder her husband, but it was the evidence of Gerry Heapes which could really seal Catherine's fate. Heapes could be a very influential witness if his evidence contained all he had outlined to the Gardaí during his many inter-views with them, and also in his unsigned written statements. But would he testify?

Gerry Heapes looked an intimidating figure as he made his entry into the witness box. More than six feet tall and built like a tank, he certainly gave the impression of a person who was well capable of looking after himself – and anyone who might be fool-ish enough to interfere with him. His direct evidence commenced.

He had first met Catherine in Finglas at the Sinn Féin advice centre. He attended the official opening of Jack White's Inn with his wife as guests of Catherine, and stayed overnight.

Some years later, he met Catherine in Finglas, and she asked him to go for a drive with him in a big white car. Conversation flowed, and it soon became apparent to him that Catherine was not happy with her lot. Tom, her husband, was making her life a misery, she told him. 'Would you be prepared to get rid of him?' she asked. 'I want him shot dead.'

He was taken completely by surprise and wasn't sure how to react, so he told her that that kind of a job takes money, lots of it. Money would be no problem, she said. On a bank holiday week-end, Tom would be carrying between £20,000 and £25,000 in cash – the pubs takings for the weekend. He thought at first that this approach was not serious, but he was beginning to realise that she was, in fact, deadly serious. He told her to leave it with him and he would get back to her.

He informed the court that he discussed her propositions with 'certain people'. He was told to get more information from her. A few weeks later, Catherine once more met him, and she drove him to the Phoenix Park. Her proposition was discussed in some detail. No one, he told her, would do what she had asked for the kind of money she was offering.

What are we talking about, she asked him? How much would it take? There would be money available, she said: there was a double insurance policy on Tom's life, and she could pay when she received payment on them. Not good enough, he told her: the money would have to be upfront. Come back to me if you can come up with it. Again, he reported back to his people.

The next journey was about three weeks later. Catherine told him that she had resolved the money issue. 'She would skim money from the takings at Jack White's, and the manager of the Blanchardstown bank would open an account, in her maiden name.' He told her to get back to him when there was money in the account.

About four or five weeks after the last meeting, they met again, and once more drove to the Phoenix Park. She took a bank book out of her bag. He didn't know the name of the bank or the amount in the account. She pointed to a name on it which she said was her maiden name. He couldn't recall the name. Whatever doubts he may have entertained about Catherine's seriousness in having her husband killed were dispelled. She was serious: she wanted Tom out of the way permanently.

What, asked Heapes, was the best way to do the job? She then drove to a house off South Circular Road, and stopped outside it. This, she told him, was Tom's first stop after leaving Jack White's Inn, to collect rent on their apartments. He would normally have an employee, a barman, with him. The barman would go to collect the rents, leaving Tom outside alone in the car. This, she added, would be the perfect place to 'do' him. No way, he told her; the street was too narrow, with cars parked on both sides. He would be noticed if that was to be the location. Perhaps if he waited in the hall for him, then it could be done there, she suggested. Again he disagreed.

His people were now treating the matter very seriously, and advised him to keep them informed of developments.

Three days later, they met again, and this time she outlined the route Tom would take on his way to the bank. If he was late for the bank, he would drive to Clonee for lunch at the Grasshopper pub, and park outside it. He would sit beside a window in the pub, from where he would have a view of the car. The bank lodgement would be in the boot. After lunch, Tom would return to the city, stopping at Kepak meat factory to collect meat for the pub.

Catherine stopped outside the Grasshopper pub, looked at him, and said: 'This would be the ideal place to do him.' From there, she drove to a side road in Phoenix Park near the Wellington Monument and pointed to the view of Islandbridge, saying: 'Tom's movements could be watched from here as he was coming from the flats, and when crossing the bridge he could be followed.' The issue of money had to be finalised, of course and after some discussion a sum of £35,000 was agreed: £10,000 up front, and £25,000 in takings from the pub. A pin could be heard falling as Heapes continued his direct evidence. This was scintillating stuff.

Events were becoming more sinister; the single-minded intent of Catherine was not only causing concern to him, but also to his people. Despite this, the meetings between them were to continue. Some days after their last meeting, she drove from the flats at South Circular Road to Islandbridge and into the Phoenix Park – the route Tom had taken on his way to the bank. From a strategic point in the Phoenix Park, she pointed to a view of Islandbridge as one approached from the flats. When Tom's car came into view, it could be followed. They travelled that route and parked outside the pub. The duration of the journey was calculated, allowing for variables such as traffic.

Outside the pub, she stated: 'I have no alibi.' But if she accompanied Tom on the day of the shooting, she could make sure that he would be late to do the banking, and they would continue on as usual to the Grasshopper pub for lunch. She would be with him as he was shot coming out of the pub. This would provide the perfect alibi: she could play the part of the grieving widow.

'This would be dangerous,' he told her. 'You could be injured during the shooting.'

'All the better,' she replied.

He asked her: 'Just how am I to get the money out of the car, as Tom would have the keys?'

No problem, she told him: 'I will get you a spare key, or you can take the keys from him when he is shot.' This coming St Patrick's weekend would be ideal for the job, she insisted. The notice is too short for such a mission, he told her. Heapes queried about the pub takings for a bank holiday weekend. The money is kept overnight at Wicklow Garda Station, and it will be in the boot of Tom's car as he sets out to bank it in Dublin, she assured him.

Heapes had become seriously troubled by the situation Catherine was trying to involve him in, and decided to opt out of the scheme. After this, they went their separate ways, and didn't meet again for almost two years.

During 1994, he and a man called Pierce Moran called to Jack White's Inn with a pre-arranged plan to try to con Catherine out of the £10,000 she had offered him up front some years previously. He would introduce Moran as a reliable and efficient contract killer, prepared to carry out her wishes to murder Tom. She approached them and, before the plan could even be put to her, informed Heapes that Tom and she had been reconciled, everything was fine, and she no longer wanted him killed.

Mr McEntee stared for a few brief seconds at Heapes, before going for the jugular. 'When Mrs Nevin approached you, why didn't you tell her: "Sorry, but killing him is out of the question?" Why didn't you tell her the IRA was not into that sort of thing, and I'm no longer in that organisation and I don't kill people?'

Heapes informed Mr McEntee that Catherine Nevin had never mentioned the IRA in any of her approaches to him. He was a member of Sinn Féin. The robbery at the cash and carry at

Fairview in 1977 was mentioned. Yes, admitted Heapes, they had been caught red-handed by the Gardaí, and the siege went on for hours before he and the gang surrendered. For his part in it, he got a ten-year sentence.

'Why did your involvement with Sinn Féin and attendance at their meetings cool?'

'Because I had given the most of twenty years to the republican movement and felt that time should now be given to my family.'

When he was asked about his reaction to being solicited to murder Tom Nevin, he replied: 'No, I didn't go to the Gardaí when she solicited me to murder her husband, simply because I have no time for them, because of the treatment meted out to me by the Special Branch over the years. In any event, I didn't think she was serious or would go ahead with it.'

'Were you not by your attitude towards Catherine leaving the door open, or offering an invitation for continuance by her?' asked Mr McEntee. 'No,' came the reply, 'I looked on it as an escape route.'

Mr McEntee moved on to the two people Heapes kept informed of Catherine's continued efforts to have him murder her husband. Heapes said that 'Redser and Macker', whom he met in the pool hall, thought that her plan to have Tom killed was a wind-up.

'What are their names?'

'I only know them as Redser and Macker,' he stated. 'They were not well known or of any importance.' However, he believed that they had a word with Catherine, advising her to stop there and then.

The continuing barrage of questions from Mr McEntee would have broken a lesser man than Heapes, but he remained cool, calm and composed. He did not over-elaborate with his answers, keeping to the point and answering in as few words as possible.

The three main witnesses for the State had completed their evidence. If it was taken on board by the jury, this evidence would go a long way towards having guilty verdicts returned. They could have been sceptical of the evidence given by the main prosecution witnesses, but corroboration of their evidence was strong and unambiguous.

Gerry Heapes was perhaps the main target of the three men approached by Catherine to murder her husband. She was no doubt influenced by his less-than-honourable past. She knew that he had a previous conviction for armed robbery, and would perhaps be a good bet to carry out the murder. She had many meetings with him, and the information he had was so accurate that it must have come from her. As a result, corroboration of his evidence was so strong as to be practically irrefutable.

Paddy McEntee, for Catherine Nevin, had done his damnedest to show Heapes, Jones and McClean as not being credible witnesses and as lacking in moral character.

The past history of these men was not an issue, and they were not facing any charges. They had held up their hands and put their less-than-rosy past on public display – to the detriment of themselves and their families. They may have been branded as thieves and rogues, but any involvement in murder was a different matter entirely. Their contact with Catherine had led the Gardaí to them. They came on board later (though not immediately) and gave every possible assistance to the investigation.

The State had now closed its case; in the investigation team, there was intense debate as to the likely outcome of the trial. There was unanimous agreement about the impression Heapes, Jones and McClean had made on the jury. Quite simply, we all felt that they had come across well, though we wondered if their previous brushes with the law would militate against the acceptance of their evidence.

30

CATHERINE IN THE WITNESS BOX

The opera's not over till the fat lady sings. The next stage in the case inevitably focused on Catherine – though she was definitely not on the flabby side.

Throughout the trial, the six men and six women of the jury were riveted to their seats as detailed evidence of the plot Catherine Nevin had hatched for years to have her husband murdered unfolded. She wanted to rid herself of the shackles she felt he had fastened tightly on her ambitions – ambitions which, when achieved, would bestow upon her new-found wealth, and the freedom to pursue her amorous pursuits of various men.

Tom was described by all who had known him as a gentle giant of a man: quiet, inoffensive, unassuming, and with a love of everything Irish, particularly Irish music and hurling. Catherine was to tell the Gardaí and her friends alike that she loved him dearly; in fact, he was her only love. The court heard a different story: the deep animosity she bore Tom (witness the fact that she had many extramarital affairs) culminated in her attempts to get three individuals to murder him, or to arrange his murder. She failed with those three – Heapes, Jones and McClean – but persisted until she got somebody to carry out her plan.

Catherine was not obliged to take the stand; if she had not done so, however, the jury would undoubtedly have regarded this as being in conflict with her claims of innocence. She would also have to face cross-examination by Peter Charlton SC.

Catherine's love of taking centre stage did not go unnoticed by the officers investigating the case. Even with the stakes so high, we felt that this was a golden opportunity which would be seized by her. Her ego was well known, but so also was her inclination to dwell on fantasy and to convince herself that it was fact. This would not suffice to sway the jury.

There was an eerie silence in court as she made her way slowly and with composure to the witness box. This was the moment everyone had been waiting for. All present were seeking tell-tale signs of emotion of apprehension – and were perhaps expecting to see a frightened woman unsure of her future or the ordeal she was about to face. On the contrary, she gave the impression of being confident and determined, seeking to right the wrong that had been done to her.

Prior to Catherine leaving her seat for the witness box, Vincent and Betty, her brother and sister, respectively, placed their hands tenderly on her shoulders and smiled gently and comfortingly at her. This was in stark contrast to Tom Nevin's family, all of whom showed their justifiable hatred of the woman making her way to the witness box. She avoided any eye contact with the Nevin family throughout the duration of the trial and gave them a wide berth outside the courtroom.

Her poise throughout the trial never wavered. Each day, on commencement of business, she seated herself in an upright position, placed her hands on both knees, and stared fixedly at the witness giving evidence. She gave not the slightest indication that she was in court charged with the murder of her husband. She was always meticulously turned out, as had been described by the newspapers, and was able to remain, at least outwardly, relaxed and at ease in the hard, timber seats when most of those present were experiencing discomfort after the lengthy sessions. It was noticeable that Catherine made no attempt to avoid photographers, who were in daily attendance, despite Judge Carroll's ruling prohibiting the use of photographs of her until the trial had run its course.

All eyes were firmly fixed on her – none more so than those of every member of the investigation team and the Nevin family. Both would share many similar feelings about this woman. The Nevins had been denied the continued existence and love of a son, brother and relative. Catherine Nevin had also made life a misery for many of the Gardaí, especially those based in Arklow – in particular Vincent Whelan and Michael Murphy. She tried to destroy their careers (and very nearly succeeded in this); she certainly made their lives, and those of their families, a living hell for years.

Facing Judge Carroll, with her hands resting on her lap, Catherine assumed a posture she would maintain throughout her direct evidence and cross-examination. She was at long last ready to tell her side of the story for the benefit of the court and the entire nation. It was 14 March, day twenty-two of the trial.

Rather than straightening his wig, Mr McEntee nudged it gently, causing it to tilt more to one side, giving a somewhat unusual placing to this most resplendent piece of headgear. He faced Catherine as he commenced his direct examination. Her replies were slow, audible, and very much focused on the questions in the beginning. As she replied to each question, Mr McEntee would glance briefly at the jury and also towards Judge Carroll, no doubt looking for a reaction.

It was evident after a few minutes of Catherine's testimony that she would include insinuations, suggestions, and far-fetched condemnations of her husband, and his activities, despite the fact that she was not being asked directly about these things. The real Catherine was surfacing.

Her first bombshell was not long in coming, and seemed to take even Mr McEntee by surprise. She had stated that 'Tom had political friends.'

'What do you mean by political friends?' Mr McEntee asked.

Catherine then dropped the clanger: 'My lord, my husband was a member of the IRA.'

Mr Charlton glanced briefly at me; I was sitting directly behind him for the duration of the trial. With a shrug of the shoulders and a shake of the head, I indicated: 'No, not so.'

She said she had first become aware of Tom's involvement in the IRA about three years after their wedding. A few times a week, Tom would come home very late. She felt that he may have been having a relationship and confronted him. They had a heart-to-heart, and he told her that 'the IRA was a part of his life, and always would be'.

'Why did you not tell anyone about this before?'

'Because, my lord, I had made Tom a solemn promise not to divulge this information to anyone.'

She claimed that IRA meetings were held regularly at the pub. She could clearly hear them arguing about money and other matters. Cars used by them were parked in the car park at the rear of the pub. There would be many cars when the meetings were held, she said.

She was, of course, trying to bring a subversive element into the fatal act, as she had not previously referred to IRA meetings at Jack White's pub. Not just ordinary meetings, but ones at which there was a great deal of heated argument about money. However, in excess of ten garda witnesses would give evidence of patrolling the area late at night and early in the morning, and never seeing anything even remotely suspicious.

Catherine said that 'Tom was interested in buying the Killinarden Inn, in Tallaght, but the asking price was high. They visited the pub on a number of occasions. Tom decided he wanted it, and a meeting was arranged in the Green Isle Hotel; this meeting was attended by Tom, herself, John Jones, a man from the North, and two other well-known republicans.' John Jones denied in evidence that he had ever attended such a meeting.

As a result of the meeting, it was decided that Tom was to put up £500,000 and would hold the title to the pub. Jones would contribute £100,000 (again, this was denied in evidence by him). Tom had £100,000, which he had got from the North; she had seen this amount written in a deposit book produced by him. Their houses at Mountshannon Road and South Circular Road were to be used as collateral.

'No, my lord, the deal wasn't finalised. Something happened between John Jones and my husband; as a result, the deal fell through. Jones and my husband had many dealings, mostly of a political nature.'

She recalled a particular incident involving her husband and John Jones, around 1985, when the Nevins were running the Barry House pub. Tom let Jones live in one of their flats rent-free. He had been there a number of weeks when she noticed a light on in the property as she passed it around 3 AM early one morning; she decided to investigate.

As she entered the house, she was met by two dangerous-looking men. One picked up a piece of glass and attacked her. She put up her hands to protect her face from the attach, and as a result two of her fingers were cut.

She phoned her husband, who told her that under no circumstances should she contact the Gardaí. She had the wounds stitched. Back at home, she related her experiences to Tom, and on his insistence they returned to the flat and collected the wires and TV components; she personally gave them to John Jones. (This was again denied by him.) It was not difficult to grasp that Catherine was trying to portray Tom as 'one of them'.

The vexatious question of the Nevins' relations with the Gardaí, in particular the Arklow-based Gardaí, was next on the agenda. The local Gardaí had been frequent customers of the pub, and were of course most welcome, she insisted. This all changed when she was obliged to make complaints against one of them to his superiors of sexual assaults on her, and also on one of the female staff, and complaints against two of them regarding corruption in relation to the granting of the restaurant licence for Jack White's. There was also the issue of a civil bill which had been taken out against her for defamation by Detective Jim McCawl. After she made the complaints, there was a complete change of attitude by the Gardaí towards the premises, herself and her husband.

Moving on to the state of their marriage, she looked at Mr McEntee and declared: 'We were happy, we had a good marriage. Tom was a good man, very quiet, and had many good qualities. His marriage was very important to him, and making it work was his number one priority. His interests were football, hurling, Irish music and playing darts. Yes, my lord, we were very happy. [But] Tom's drinking caused some problems: he was an alcoholic.' She was pulling no punches.

What were the sleeping arrangements between you and your husband? she was asked. 'Tom and I had occupied separate bedrooms after we got married. If we wanted to make love, there were plenty of bedrooms available to facilitate this.'

Are you saying you did make love? counsel enquired. 'Yes, frequently, my lord, yes.' Her husband and she had last made love on 28 February, his birthday. I heard one person whisper: 'He must have thought all his birthdays had come together.'

She went on to say: 'It is certainly not true that I had any kind of a sexual relationship with Tom Kennedy. His family were very good friends with Tom and myself. There was nothing more to it . . . . Tom Kennedy only stayed late in the pub on rare occasions and, other than on the night of his retirement party, never later than 3 AM.'

Allegations of an inappropriate relationship with Judge O'Buachalla were simply not true, she said. 'He and his wife were very good friends of Tom and [me] . . . No, my lord, Judge O'Buachalla never had a set of keys for the pub; he had no need for them . . . . No, I never had male company with me at our properties in Dublin.'

To be a good liar, one has to have a good memory. Direct evidence would have been a doddle for Catherine. She would have been well-rehearsed in advance of entering the witness box. Cross-examination was unlikely to be an easy ride for her, however, as she faced one of the sharpest minds in court practice and procedure.

On the morning of 16 March 2000, I, with Detective Gerry McKenna, was making the tedious daily pilgrimage from Gorey to the Four Courts. We were discussing how Catherine would stand up to the cross-examination which was to start at 11 that morning. We felt that she had not done herself any favours when casting Tom as a member of the IRA, as well as a raging alcoholic. How could she expect that anyone would believe her previous declarations of undying love for him after that? We felt sure that Mr Charlton was chomping at the bit, awaiting his opportunity to cross-examine her.

Then, the RTÉ 10 o'clock news announced that Catherine Nevin had been removed from home by ambulance that morning and taken to St James's Hospital, Dublin. No further details were available at that time.

I glanced at Gerry. 'Good fuck, what next?' I exclaimed. Gerry wondered if she was dead, before breaking into hysterical laughter. Will this trial ever finish? we wondered.

The Four Courts was packed with concerned parties and onlookers alike. No one had precise details of what had happened, as we awaited the arrival of the judge and both sets of counsel.

Facing Judge Carroll, Mr McEntee informed her that he simply did not know what had happened or what the circumstances of Catherine's removal to hospital were. The judge and Mr Charlton were not amused by this latest development. There was perhaps a simple and acceptable explanation, but it was widely felt that this was yet another of Catherine's calculated ploys to gain the jury's sympathy. A solicitor was dispatched to the hospital, and the Gardaí set in motion their own inquiries.

Judge Carroll was left with no option but to dismiss the jury for the day. She also imposed reporting restrictions. St Patrick's weekend followed.

On Monday, back in court, Mr McEntee informed Judge Carroll that his client was still detained in hospital, suffering from the effects of the ingestion of noxious substances, the type not yet known. She was in the care of the hospital consultant who was on duty when she was admitted. She had also been examined by two other consultants, one of whom had been engaged by the defence.

That same day, Dr David Breen, medical registrar of St James's Hospital, attended court and outlined the result of a toxicology report carried out on Catherine. Three drugs had been taken; two of them were significant: Dalmaine, a sedative which could only be obtained on prescription, and Tylex, a painkiller containing paracetamol and codeine, an opiate. The third substance was Spironolact One, a diuretic used to reduce swelling in the legs.

The level of paracetamol found was 45 micrograms per milliliter – a potentially toxic level. Had they been taken one hour before detection, they would not be toxic. He and the other consultants were of the view that Catherine would be able to resume her evidence that Wednesday, 22 March.

Catherine Nevin was back in the witness box as promised by Dr Breen on Wednesday, a full seven days after finishing her direct evidence.

'I want an explanation,' demanded Judge Carroll, who gave the impression that she was anything but pleased by this most recent turn of events. Paddy McEntee SC felt that it wasn't necessary to go into the reasons for Catherine's absence from the court. The look from Judge Carroll made it clear what she thought of this.

Catherine looked the worse for wear as she began to explain the reasons for her enforced absence. Her features looked gaunt and her voice was barely audible. Would this be enough to convince everyone present of the nightmare she had experienced since her last appearance in court? She looked meekly and almost apologetically at Judge Carroll, before beginning her story.

She said that when the court's business had finished, Vincent, her brother, had driven her to her accommodation at Mountshannon Road. They had arrived there at approximately 7.30 PM. Vincent went to his own accommodation, which was only a few hundred yards away, and she entered her apartment.

She noticed that the mortise lock on the front door and the lock on her flat door were unlocked. Having entered the flat, she had a feeling that someone was in it. As she attempted to turn on the light, she tripped over the feet of a man who was sitting on the couch. She recognised him as an associate of her husband's. She didn't know him by name but over the years had seen him on numerous occasions with her husband. He was about forty years of age and wearing an anorak.

She was terrified by the presence of this intruder. 'You are naming people in court you shouldn't be naming, causing problems for people. You will now stop and name no others,' the intruder warned her.

The intruder pulled tablets from his pocket and forced her to take them. She didn't know how many, or what they were. 'He gave me something white to drink, [it] tasted like milk. After he left, I got sick, violently sick, then I got sick a second time. After that, everything was a blank until I awoke in hospital.'

Vincent arrived to collect her at 9.30 that morning. He knocked on the front door and got no response. Eventually, another tenant answered the door, and admitted Vincent and one of the detectives who was on duty outside the house.

Catherine was lying on a couch, dressed only in a pink pyjamas. How was it that she was wearing a pyjamas when she was found, apparently unconscious, and not the suit she had worn when she had been confronted by the intruder?

When the ambulance driver arrived at the flat, there was a smell and presence of vomit. Spirit bottles were on the table, as were some prescription medicines. The ambulance driver got the impression that Catherine was feigning unconsciousness.

While examining her flat, the Gardaí noticed a bottle of washing-up liquid. Vomit samples from the flat were examined at the Forensic Science Laboratory by Dr John Power, who found that the vomit had a soaplike odour and contained a fatty-liquid content. The implication was that she had made herself vomit by drinking washing-up liquid. Vegetable oil is one of the main components of washing-up liquid, and she could have eaten fatty foods that evening; the tests were inconclusive.

Robert Sinnott, who occupied the flat next to Catherine's, heard movement in Catherine's flat around 7 AM. Normally he would hear Catherine's movements between 7.45 and 8 AM. (Gardaí interviewed many residents and neighbours about the alleged attack on Catherine: over twenty statements were taken, but nothing of relevance was ascertained.) The mortise lock on the front door is not always kept locked, as tenants come and go on a regular basis, and as often as not they fail to lock the door.

The biggest problem for Catherine lay in the fact that the intruder was able to enter and leave the flat without alerting the Gardaí who were on duty outside it. Why did she not struggle when the medication was forced on her? For all she knew, it could have been poison. There was no evidence of any struggle. The only interesting aspect of the flat, other than the bottles of spirits and medication, was the messy state it was in. This was in stark contrast with the attention to detail regarding her own personal appearance on a daily basis.

So ended the tale of Catherine's latest traumatic experience, which she hoped would gain her much-needed sympathy and support from the jury. The pros and cons of her fairy tale had been discussed by defence and prosecution counsel alike, but in the absence of the jury. It was not intended to introduce any of it in evidence. The jury would be aware only that Catherine had been hospitalised.

Catherine's cross-examination began with her conversation

with Donacha Long, the carpet fitter. He had given evidence that he had been fitting carpets at the pub the week prior to the murder and that Catherine had told him that Tom was 'a queer', and that she was going to 'have him done'. She denied that this conversation ever took place.

The night of the murder, and the staff's preparations for the disco in Arklow, was the next matter to be raised. Several of the staff had given evidence that Catherine had forbade them to stay on the premises that night, and that this was something she had never previously done. She had said this some weeks prior to the murder and on the night of the murder. She strongly denied ever issuing that instruction to the girls.

She couldn't describe the intruder (or intruders) because the light was off. 'No it wasn't, because the Gardaí had given evidence that it was on,' Mr Charlton countered. 'Perhaps they were lying,' she remarked.

Suddenly, another well-known garda officer was introduced out of the blue by Catherine, in reply to a question by Mr Charlton. She stated: 'I can't remember if Tom Kennedy ever came to darts matches with me. I do remember Superintendent Bill Ryan being with me on one occasion.' Superintendent Ryan had been the superintendent in charge of Wicklow Garda District at or around the same time as Tom Kennedy was the inspector there. 'Tom was away on that occasion,' she said. Which Tom she was referring to is unclear.

The questions were coming fast and furious, and were having the desired effect. The mask of composure and credibility was beginning to slip; this was reflected in the ambiguous nature of her replies.

'You told your bank manager, in the presence of Rose and Theresa Nevin back at the pub after the funeral, that you had been reading in bed when the intruder burst in,' stated Mr Charlton.

'I have no recollection of ever saying that.'

'Why did you not press the panic button in your bedroom? It

was within reach and could easily have been activated, even by a gentle push on the button?'

'I didn't know it was there.'

'Gardaí McAndew, Cummiskey and Collins have informed the court that the door was ajar by about six inches when they first arrived at the scene, and they were able without any difficulty to open it fully. Why couldn't you?'

'I tried very hard but just couldn't open it.'

The next question – and her answer to it – really put the cat among the pigeons. 'Did you not think of looking for Tom, were you not concerned for his safety, or did you think of calling out for his help? After all, he was the only person in the place that could help.'

'It never crossed my mind. Tom had always told me that in the event of a break-in, I should not worry about him, as he could and would look after himself.'

She queried the truthfulness of the evidence given by Mr McHugh, the assistant garda commissioner. Her conversation with him was different to the evidence given by him. 'I cannot determine or influence what other people say,' she stated.

In reference to her husband's alleged membership of the IRA, and to him being an alcoholic, she replied: 'I don't know if the IRA were content to have an alcoholic as a member; I know nothing about them. I am not a member and do not support them.'

Regarding Pat Russell, alias John Ferguson, she said: 'I only got in touch with him because Tom asked me to.' She never told Russell she wanted to buy Tom's share in the pub, or that he was an alcoholic, and not pulling his weight. She did not tell Detective Joe Collins that she did not know the identity of John Ferguson, because he never asked her.

Her refusal to give a statement when asked by Detective Sergeant O'Brien and Detective Collins was put to her. Her answer, if true, would have serious implications for them. 'I did not tell Detective Collins and Sergeant O'Brien anything because it was dangerous to make a statement, as it would be doctored.'

They were, by inference, added to her ever-growing list of perjurers – if Catherine was telling the truth, the whole truth, and nothing but the truth.

She never told members of the staff or Mrs Nora Finnerty (a relative of Tom's) that she and Tom were separating. The staff members who had given this evidence were Janessa Phelan and Anne Marie Finnerty (the latter being the daughter of Nora, and the niece of Tom Nevin).

According to Catherine, Willie McClean was lying when he stated that they had had a sexual affair lasting eighteen months, that he had been at the official opening of the pub, and that he had stayed there overnight, and at weekends. She said that he had never visited her in hospital; she had never asked him to kill her husband or arrange his murder, or that she wanted the murder carried out at the flats or on Tom's way to the bank.

She denied ever asking John Jones to kill her husband or to get someone to do it. She didn't tell him that Tom was violent and beat her up on occasions. Her husband had told her to take down his phone number, but she didn't explain why. She couldn't explain how Jones knew of their banking arrangements, or her plans for making improvements to the pub in order to attract truckers who were traveling en route to and from Rosslare. She never told him that the two men who attacked her in the flat were SAS men. He was a very close friend of her husband, and they had many dealings together, mostly of a political nature.

John Jones was regarded so highly by her husband that he would be a silent partner in the Killinarden Inn pub, should the intended purchase by Tom and herself go through. There was an involvement north of the border in this intended purchase, and £100,000 was to be provided by contacts of Jones, or by him personally.

'No, my lord, I never asked Gerry Heapes to kill my husband or get his organisation to kill my husband.'

In fact, her most often repeated reply to the questions put to her in cross-examination was: 'No, my lord.'

She said: 'Tom Kennedy's wife, Mary, hadn't been in the pub since about 1993.'

'Could it have been in the 1980s?' asked Mr Charlton.

'No, my lord, no way,' came the reply.

'Your allegation to the court, that Tom, your husband, was a member of the IRA – is this not character assassination of a man not capable of reply?' asked Mr Charlton.

'Tom was a member of the IRA; I wasn't,' she asserted.

She blamed Tom for crossing out the name and phone number of Gerry Heapes on the reverse side of the page in her diary/phone index book. She admitted crossing the details out on the front of the page, but only because Tom had been furious when he saw the entry.

In her statement to the Gardaí, she said that she had spoken to the raiders, telling them where her jewellery was. In court, she said she had never said anything to them after they had burst into her bedroom.

She told Detective Collins that the knife the raiders had used was short; in court, she said it was long.

Gerry Heapes had given evidence about the big white car she had been driving when she had solicited him to kill her husband, and accompanying her in it to the Phoenix Park and Clonee. Her reply was: 'I never drove a white car in which he was a passenger.' They did own a white Opel Vectra at that time.

As the trial neared its end, and Catherine was enduring her last few minutes in the witness box, one could not but be enthralled by her remarkable self-control. Not once did she display any emotion suggestive of guilt, anxiety or embarrassment. On the contrary, she gave the impression of being completely relaxed and at ease with the situation.

The Nevins were called to give evidence in relation to Catherine's allegations that Tom was involved with the IRA. They didn't want the limelight, and were apprehensive about giving evidence in such a charged atmosphere. On the other hand, their sister-in-law, Catherine Nevin, had branded their brother as a terrorist by implying that he was a member of the IRA, and had also suggested that he was an alcoholic, a homosexual and a wife-beater. They gave forceful evidence about Tom Nevin, implying that her evidence was so far off the mark as to be disgusting. Tom's first wife, June O'Flanagan, strongly rebutted the allegation that Tom was a homosexual. She described him as a gentle, kind, hard-working man, and attributed the failure of their marriage entirely to herself.

Giving evidence in court was a traumatic experience for the Nevins and June O'Flanagan, and many people in the courtroom were in tears. As they later proclaimed: 'It was difficult, but it was worth it.'

Catherine's posture and gait as she walked purposely from the witness box to the body of the court was not that of a woman who had undergone a demanding and articulate cross-examination by one of the foremost senior counsels in the land. In fact, she gave the impression of total defiance and steely determination as her ordeal drew to an end.

The plan which she had nurtured over many years to murder her husband, or cause him to be murdered, was seen by her as being foolproof. Had she convinced the jury of her innocence? She had undoubtedly made an impression on them, but would it be the one she was hoping for?

31

THE CLOSING SPEECH FOR THE PROSECUTION

M r Tom O'Connell BL made the closing speech for the prosecution to the jury, outlining the relevant evidence they had heard throughout this long and difficult trial. The speech lasted more than four hours.

He referred to the plethora of evidence which had been placed before the jury by the witnesses, including members of staff at Jack White's Inn, garda experts, members of the garda investigation team, the state pathologist, a judge, a retired garda inspector, and members of the deceased's family.

He said that the jury should carefully consider Catherine's many lies, inaccuracies and unsupported evidence. She had refused to make a written statement or to answer even one question during her forty-eight-hour detention.

Was Caroline Strahan's evidence that she had seen Catherine and Tom Kennedy in bed a lie? Or Willie McClean's evidence that he had had an eighteen-month-long affair with her? Were Willie McClean, John Jones and Gerry Heapes lying when they independently gave precise and identical particulars of her efforts to solicit them to murder her husband, or cause him to be murdered?

As in all crimes, there has to be a motive. Catherine had many, including her desire to be rid of Tom, and to gain complete ownership of Jack White's pub and the couple's other properties. On Tom's death, Catherine would inherit property worth well in excess of £1,000,000 – not an inconsiderable sum in 1996. Tom was also regarded as a nuisance, and a hindrance to her sexual relationships. With him out of the picture, the way would be clear for her amorous activities. 'Anyone could have her but me', Tom had stated. She had schemed and planned for years to obtain the services of a hit man. Mistakenly, she believed that Gerry Heapes, John Jones and Willie McClean would be enticed by the lure of approximately £20,000 to carry out her evil plan. Eventually, she succeeded in having her dreams fulfilled.

Evidence from Dr Harbison, the state pathologist, and garda technical experts suggested that Tom Nevin was shot at close range – an indication that he knew the assassin or was surprised. He didn't put up a struggle, as he was holding a biro in his writing hand, and his spectacles were in the reading position.

Mr O'Connell also made reference to the noise and smell – emanating from the kitchen – Catherine got in her bedroom. The problem is that the powder used to propel the fatal shot was nitro cellulose, which is smokeless and practically odourless. This smell could not under any circumstances have been detected in Catherine's bedroom. The only way Catherine could possibly have got the smell is if she had been present in the kitchen when the fatal shot was fired, or immediately afterwards. During the firearms tests carried out by the Gardaí, shots from the kitchen were also easily identifiable as gunshots.

There was no forced entry – leading to the conclusion that the intruders had been admitted by someone who was already on the premises, or had been concealed on the premises prior to the murder. Catherine was the only known person on the premises prior to, and at the time, the murder was committed. 'A contrived scene' was how Assistant Commissioner McHugh had described it.

There was no appearance of a systematic search having been carried out. The manner in which the jewellery was found lends substance to the theory of the scene being contrived.

Why was the cash in each of the cash registers not taken, and why were the bundles of notes, amounting to £4,000, in another safe left behind by the raiders? Armed with a deadly weapon, they came intent on getting Catherine's jewellery, killed her husband, and left without these valuable possessions. Could such blundering idiots be regarded as serious robbers? Why the necessity to kill him? He put up no struggle and was no threat to anyone confronting him with a shotgun. He had been sitting on a stool doing the books for the day's takings, and sipping from his half-pint glass of Guinness. The ammunition used, sufficient to bring down big game, would cause instant death, and suggests that he had been killed by a contract killer.

Catherine had been intent on ensuring that no one would be staying on the premises the night of the murder. She had indicated this to staff some weeks prior to the event, and again prior to them leaving for the disco that night. She was also to refuse a couple bed and breakfast for that night, having one of the staff tell them that there were no vacancies, when in fact all the bedrooms were available.

In summing up, Tom O'Connell stated: 'It would be up to you, the jury, to decide the guilt or innocence of the accused, having due regard to the evidence placed before you in this case.'

32

THE CLOSING SPEECH FOR THE DEFENCE

Paddy McEntee, wig still slightly tilted to one side, was facing the jury as he began his closing speech. He took in excess of ten hours for his final address to the jury.

Mr McEntee's cross-examinations had been so intense and probing that some witnesses had found it difficult to react as questions were put to them. This is perhaps understandable when taking into account the tender age of the young girls employed at Jack White's who were called to give evidence. Their evidence was mostly focused on Catherine, her husband Tom, Judge O'Buachalla, and former garda inspector Tom Kennedy. Not one of the staff had supplied any direct evidence to link Catherine with John Jones, Gerry Heapes and Willie McClean, or her efforts in soliciting them to murder her husband.

McEntee touched on the credibility of Jones, Heapes and McClean. They were, he reminded the jury, convicted criminals, and Jones and Heapes had openly stated in evidence that they were members of Sinn Féin.

Why, he wondered, did they not take decisive action when they were propositioned, rather than years later, after Tom Nevin had been murdered? They knew that what was being suggested by Catherine was an evil crime. Why, when they were in possession of information such as they had, did they not approach the Gardaí, rather than wait for the Gardaí to contact them. Why did Gerard Heapes decline to sign his written statement to the Gardaí?

Catherine Nevin had been the subject of much criticism concerning her extramarital affairs, but her morals were not the subject of the trial. Each question put to her during her many hours in the witness box had been fully and truthfully answered. Other than the evidence of Heapes, Jones and McClean, what other evidence had the State produced to justify the jury returning a guilty verdict or verdicts of guilty as charged?

These were some of McEntee's submissions on why the jury should return not-guilty verdicts. He told them: 'If you entertain any doubt about my client being guilty, any doubt at all . . . then the law states my client is entitled to the benefit of that doubt.'

Mr McEntee's attention to detail and recollection of previous evidence throughout the trial was nothing short of awesome. His physical and mental endurance, which must have been tried to the limit, can best be likened to that of a marathon runner.

Judge Carroll's charge to the jury was lengthy, highly articulate, and informative in a common-sense way. It touched on every aspect of evidence the jury had heard: the many inconsistencies in Catherine's evidence compared to that given by the Gardaí, forensic experts, members of the staff at Jack White's Inn, June O'Flaherty, members of the Nevin family and, most importantly of all, John Jones, Gerry Heapes and Willie McClean. They should, she advised them, consider these matters carefully and completely before arriving at any decision.

So ended the longest trial in Irish legal history. It had taken a total of sixty-one days in all. The jury had to choose who was telling the truth. They retired at 3.10 PM on Friday 7 April 2000. Catherine had tried, unsuccessfully, to get eye contact with them during the closing speeches and the charge to the jury by Judge

Carroll. In fact, this was a noticeable feature throughout the trial.

There was a weariness evident on the faces of the main pro-tagonists as the jury made their way from the court to the jury room. Everyone seemed glad that the curtain had finally fallen on the arguments and counter-arguments. Though they did not know it as they made their way from the body of the courtroom, the jury was to start deliberations which were to be amongst the longest in Irish legal history.

In the beginning, we all thought that guilty verdicts would be returned. This was to change as day one progressed to day five; many believed that it would not take five days to find her guilty. What no one wanted was a hung jury, and perhaps another trial.

The weekend came and passed. Saturday was a glorious spring day, where a walk in the open would be much more desirable than sitting in a packed, stuffy courtroom. On Sunday, the courtroom was still packed to capacity. At midday, the jury was called by Judge Carroll, who asked them: 'Have you reached a verdict on any of the counts on which you have all agreed?' The foreperson replied 'No.' The judge then informed them that she would accept a majority verdict, and the jury returned to their room. The wait continued. Monday came and went, and still no verdict had been returned. A final decision of 'not guilty' seemed likely.

33

THE VERDICT

On Tuesday 11 April 2000, the court was packed minutes after the entrance door had been opened to the public. As the lunch break was announced, hopes were fading that this would be 'D-Day'.

I was having a cigarette with Mr McEntee shortly before the jury returned that fateful evening. Out of earshot of anyone else, McEntee suggested to me: 'Ye will be drinking champagne this evening.' We returned to the courtroom, and shortly afterwards came the long-awaited announcement: 'The jury are returning.' The time was 6.30 PM.

The jury had spent four consecutive nights in their hotel room, and their deliberations had taken five days – a record twenty-nine hours and thirty minutes. They had sat through forty-two days in court, and had listened to direct evidence from, and cross-examination of, 180-plus witnesses. You could hear a pin drop as the six men and six women walked slowly and solemnly to their seats.

Catherine's composure seemed incredible as she awaited the verdict on each of the four charges. She retained the fixed, arrogant stare she had maintained throughout the trial.

The tension was unbearable. I quickly glanced around the confines of the Central Criminal Court and made eye contact with Joe Collins and Fergus O'Brien. They seemed tense, but Joe gave me a wink and smiled confidently.

As the verdicts were read out, there was complete silence as the reality of what was being heard sank in.

Count number one: 'The murder of her husband Tom Nevin on 19 March 1996, at Jack White's Inn, Brittas Bay, County Wicklow.'

'Guilty by a unanimous verdict.'

Count number two: 'Soliciting John Jones in 1989 to murder her husband.'

'Guilty by a majority verdict of eleven to one.'

Count number three: 'Soliciting Gerry Heapes in 1990 to murder her husband.'

'Guilty by a unanimous verdict.'

Count number four: 'Soliciting William McClean to murder her husband in 1990.'

'Guilty by a majority verdict of eleven to one.'

There was silence, and disbelief, as the fourth and final verdict was read out.

The jury, by their verdicts, had accepted the evidence of John Jones, Gerard Heapes and William McClean. They had also accepted the evidence of the Gardaí, the forensic experts, and numerous civilians, including the staff at Jack White's pub.

They had rejected in its entirety Catherine Nevin's evidence, together with her damning lack of cooperation with the Gardaí, and had also recognised the many lies unearthed in her cross-examination by Peter Charlton SC. Most importantly, they had accepted that Catherine Nevin bore her husband dangerous ill will, and had for years tried unsuccessfully to have him killed. She eventually succeeded in her solicitations, culminating in the murder on 19 March 1996.

Judge Carroll, after the verdicts had been announced, told

them: 'The media have seen fit to comment on the fact that the jury had spent four nights in the comfort of a hotel during the trial. If anyone thought this was more than you deserved, then they, the media, did not appreciate the sacrifices or disruption to your lives this trial has caused. I exempt you from any further jury service for the rest of your lives.'

Showing signs of emotion, she addressed Catherine Nevin. 'I do not intend to give you any lecture. You had your husband assassinated not once but twice; once in life, and in death by assassinating his character.' She delivered the only sentence open to her: a mandatory life imprisonment.

A mighty weight had at last been lifted from the shoulders of the Nevin family, and it must have been sweet music to their ears to hear Judge Carroll's comments. She had stated: 'I hope that his family will take some consolation in these verdicts.' She rose from her seat and left the confines of the courtroom, thus bringing to a close one of the most talked-about murders and trials in the history of the Irish State.

The Nevin family had made the long journey from Galway to the Four Courts for the duration of the trial on a daily basis. Now the good name of their beloved son, brother and relative had been fully vindicated and restored.

After the verdict was announced, the Nevin family rushed forward and proudly embraced many of the Gardaí who had played such a huge part in the investigation. Detective Sergeant Fergus O'Brien and Detective Joe Collins were rightly singled out for special attention. Their contributions had been immense. Discovering the name and phone number of Gerry Heapes in Catherine's diary had put in motion a chain of events which would eventually lead to Catherine Nevin's conviction for the murder, and soliciting the murder, of Tom Nevin.

In complete contrast, Catherine's sister Betty and her brother Vincent were shocked as the guilty verdicts against their sister were read out. They each placed a hand tenderly and lovingly on

Catherine's shoulder, and tried as best they could to lend support. Both had become well known to the investigation team. Suffice it to say that I endorse fully and unequivocally the sentiments of the local community where the Scullys lived: 'The best neighbours one could have: honest, hard-working, decent people, who are well respected and loved in their neighbourhood.'

There was a spring in my step, and that of my staff, as we exited the Four Courts to be greeted by TV crews and the assembled media. I gave some brief interviews, expressing my relief at the verdicts, for which the investigation team had worked so tirelessly, and had secured against all the odds. I was especially happy for the entire Nevin family, 'who had endured such pain and heartache since 19 March 1996. Hopefully, they will in time come to terms with the tragic loss of their beloved son and brother.'

The Nevin family exited the Four Courts accompanied by a spokesperson who handed a prepared statement to the media. They expressed relief and joy at the verdicts, which fully restored the good name of Tom Nevin. The Gardaí came in for special mention, for the kindness, understanding, co-operation and sincerity they had shown towards the family from day one.

Still inside the courtroom, being comforted by her brother Vincent and sister Betty, sat Catherine Nevin, awaiting removal to her new home, Mountjoy Prison. Catherine was seen taking a ring from her finger and handing it to her sister Betty – the significance of which is not understood. As she was escorted from the courtroom, one could not but wonder at how she would cope with life in prison.

Those who remained to witness her being led from the courthouse to the van which would take her to Mountjoy Prison, to serve her sentence of life imprisonment, were shocked and amazed at her continued display of arrogance and lack of emotion. No tears, no smile, just a steely, fixed stare to remind everyone that, even in defeat, here stood before them a woman of status and quality, who had been ostracised and unfairly treated by the establishment. She would appeal this outrageous verdict, as she saw it, to the highest court in the land and, if necessary, in Europe.

Did she realise, as she was being driven away, that she had become only the sixth woman in the history of the state to be convicted of murder?

34

CATHERINE'S NEW RESIDENCE

Catherine's new home hardly represents how most people imagine a place of incarceration. The women's wing of Mountjoy was completely refurbished in the late 1990s, at a cost of in excess of £13.5 million. Prisons may conjure up visions of run-down, shabby buildings, but modern times have also produced modern prisons.

Catherine is housed in one of eight new self-contained apartments, which she shares with other inmates. She has at her disposal cooking facilities, and an area set aside for washing and ironing clothes. The doors and windows in her apartment are just that: there is no evidence of iron bars securing them, nor are there any other visible security measures to be seen in the apartment. The prison has educational facilities. She would no doubt avail of some of the academic courses available to her during her incarceration.

Her fellow inmates differ greatly from those she regarded as personal friends during her stewardship of Jack White's Inn. They include drug traffickers and those serving life sentences, to mention just a few.

Her day begins at 8 AM; breakfast is available in the communal eating area. Lunch is at 12.45 PM and tea at 4.45 PM. Supper is provided at 7.30 PM and lock-up time is usually 10 PM.

Debate continues as to whether Catherine Nevin should remain incarcerated for the rest of her natural life. Certain categories of crime, such as murder, greatly offend and disturb society. This repugnance is felt even more sharply when the perpetrator is a woman, and the victim is her husband.

Although Catherine Nevin was entitled to apply for parole in 2007, she did not: she regards an application for parole as tantamount to an admission of guilt. She has always maintained her innocence and is intent on pursuing all avenues of appeal, right up to the European Court of Justice.

Many studies have been undertaken to try to determine why women become involved in the act of murder. Many suggest that there have to be mitigating circumstances: a suffering spouse who has reached breaking point as a result of domestic violence, cruelty, alcoholism, drugs, extramarital affairs, or even jealousy.

Pat Kenny, RTÉ and *The Late Late Show* were to be disappointed the Friday night after the trial, as it was anticipated that Catherine would be released and would be a guest on his show. Her conviction was to change those plans – and thwart Catherine's ambitions to display her beauty and intelligence on the show with the highest ratings in the country.

35

THE AFTERMATH

The media would have a field day. No longer bound by the orders imposed by Judge Carroll, they could tell the story as they saw it. The prominent personalities frequently mentioned during the trial, Judge Donnacha O'Buachalla, and Garda Inspector Tom Kennedy, also received much media attention after the guilty verdicts had been returned. Judge O'Buachalla had openly and freely declared that he had 'an excellent relationship with both Catherine and Tom Nevin'. However, Jeanie Murphy, the cleaner in Jack White's, told the Gardaí: 'I heard Tom Nevin fucking and blinding the judge over the phone, telling him to fuck off, that he knew what was going on.' Other staff members were to say that Tom had no time for the judge and couldn't stand him.

Media reporting of the trial continued to be sensational. Some of the headlines the day after Catherine Nevin was found guilty read:

GUILTY, GUILTY, GUILTY, GUILTY; CATHERINE NEVIN JAILED FOR LIFE
Irish Independent, 12 April 2000

FACES OF A KILLER

'When told her husband was dead, Nevin said, "I just feel so sick, I was terrified, I was numb, I didn't want to believe it, it just couldn't possibly have happened . . . I just wish I was dead as well."'

Irish Examiner, 12 April 2000

(The paper had nine pictures of Catherine Nevin on the same page.)

THE TRAGIC TRIAL THAT BECAME A SORDID SOAP

'The friends, the lovers, and the Black Widow. It's the sordid yet gripping story of a ruthless woman who didn't stop at murder, her tragic husband who never realised what she was capable of, a respectable judge who should have known better, and a senior garda officer who was too often seen at her side.

'Neither Judge O'Buachalla nor the retired Garda Inspector Tom Kennedy were widely recognisable except, ironically, to those who may have had a brush with the law, but their relative anonymity began to evaporate when they were seen lunching with Catherine Nevin. Even after she was charged, the three of them continued to meet in a pub in Wicklow town, one Monday each month, when Judge O'Buachalla had finished his court business. It seems likely that he would have expected at that stage to be called as a witness in the murder trial, and therefore might have considered absenting himself from any hearing relating to the accused woman. . . . Catapulted into headline news for granting her a pub licence in his chambers after she had been charged with her husband's murder, it now emerges that Judge O'Buachalla had made a statement to the murder investigation team, seventeen months earlier, in April 1996.'

Irish Independent, 15 April 2000

BLUEPRINT FOR AN EVENING'S VILE BUTCHERY
'A killer brought to justice; Catherine Nevin, who ought never to be freed, gives an insight into female violence that is often too terrifying to contemplate. . . . Life should mean exactly that – life.'
Sunday Independent, 16 April 2000

NEVIN PUB IS NEW MECCA FOR SICK TOURISTS
'Streams of visitors stop for pictures outside murder spot.'
Sunday People, 16 April 2000

JUDGE'S ROLE IN NEVIN PUB LICENCE CONTROVERSY QUESTIONED
'Fine Gael spokesman on Justice, Mr Jim Higgins TD, yesterday called on Judge O'Buachalla to "stand aside" while his granting of a pub licence to Catherine Nevin in 1997 is investigated. Mr Higgins accused the judge of "sleight of judicial hand".

'In a statement made yesterday, 13 April, Judge O'Buachalla said the application was made in open court.

'Mr Ahern, the Taoiseach, replying, stated: "Early this morning the Minister asked for three separate reports. He cannot say or do any more until he receives them."'
Irish Times, 14 April 2000

36

SLEEPING DOGS

Judge O'Buachalla had issued a pub licence in the sole name of Catherine Nevin for Jack White's pub, two months after she had been charged with the murder of her husband. I took exception to the manner in which the licence was issued, which I believed was an abuse of legal process, and reported it to the state solicitor for Wicklow and Garda Headquarters. I had a number of reasons for taking this course of action:

> I did not receive the statutory written notice of intent to move the application. I was the garda officer in charge of the district and this was an essential condition in all applications under the Liquor Licensing Laws.

> It was an ex-parte application.

> The application was not in open court; it was a private hearing in the judge's chambers.

> The correct procedure would have been to apply for an ad-interim transfer, followed by a confirmation of transfer.

> There was no written notice sent to the district court clerk.

The Constitution provides that justice must be administered in public, except where a specific law allows otherwise. Applications for pub licences must be held in open court.

This was an issue involving not only the Gardaí, but also the Court Service, the Revenue Commissioners and the judiciary. It was considered to be of such a serious nature that it was raised in Dáil Éireann. As a result, three separate inquiries were ordered by the justice minister, John O'Donoghue: one by the president of the district court, one by the CEO of the district court clerks, and one by the garda commissioner. The findings were awaited with interest by myself and all other parties involved, not least the Nevins.

I became keenly aware that the results of the reports ordered by the minister of justice on 18 April 2000 had not been made public even several years after Catherine had been charged with the murder of her husband. The licence had to be regularised in order to permit Catherine to continue running the business and to keep the licence alive, should she decide to sell the premises. The Nevin family were, to put it mildly, incensed at what they saw as unlawful and improper procedure being followed.

In the file I forwarded to the state solicitor for Wicklow, and to my own superiors, I outlined what I saw as 'an appalling miscarriage of justice . . . without precedent in law'. I urged the law officers to take steps to rectify this situation.

After I retired from An Garda Síochána in January 2004, Catherine Nevin – and the pub licence for Jack White's Inn – rarely occupied my thoughts until St Patrick's Day 2008, when the issue came up in conversation with a former colleague. 'Just what was the outcome of the inquiries?' asked my friend. For the first time since I had retired, the matter once more came to fascinate me, albeit this time for different reasons. I had not been informed, either in writing or verbally, of the outcome of the four inquiries set up by Minister O'Donoghue. He had told Dáil Éireann on 18 April 2000 that he was in possession of written reports from the garda commissioner and the chief executive of the Courts Service on the matter. Mr Smithwicks, president of the district court, did not complete his inquiries. The report by Mr Frank Murphy, judge of the Supreme Court, was forwarded to Minister O'Donoghue on 23 November 2000. I had seen none of these documents.

My report was forwarded to the Wicklow state solicitor and the garda authorities in October 1997. Thus, there was a seven-year gap between my report and my retirement in January 2004. Suddenly, my interest in the matter was rekindled, and my suspicious mind went into overdrive.

There must be a logical explanation for this failure to inform me of the outcome of the inquiries, I thought. This was something I was not prepared to ignore any longer, though I was strongly advised by some of my former colleagues to let sleeping dogs lie. If the licence had not been issued on 29 September 1997, or at the latest the following day, then it would have lapsed, leaving the premises unlicensed, and debarred by law from trading.

By my stance on the matter, I was pointing the finger of suspicion at a judge. I had been quoted in the press on 14 April 2000 as saying that the manner in which the pub licence had been granted was 'unlawful and without precedent in law'. However, the Murphy Report was later to conclude that it was an abuse of legal process.

Judge O'Buachalla had publicly stated that 'the application was moved and granted in open court'. It most definitely was not, and I stated so in my report. Why was the application moved and granted at Wexford District Court, and not at Arklow, where it should have been dealt with? No explanation for this has been proffered. Why was this matter dealt with as an ex-parte application, and where is the relevant law to support this approach? Why were neither the superintendent in charge of Gorey nor the court clerks given the required written notice of the application? Without such notice, there was no application before the court, so nothing could be granted.

Despite these irregularities, and notwithstanding the fact that reservations had been expressed to him by District Court Clerks Liam Sexton and Andy Cullen, Judge O'Buachalla granted the licence. Why was no notice of the application given? This is a question the Nevin family feel strongly about. Had they received notice of an application being moved by Catherine Nevin, they would have exercised their legal and constitutional right and objected, on the grounds of her character; so too would I.

On 13 April 2000, Jim Higgins TD took the assembled members of the Dáil by surprise when he requested an adjournment to discuss a matter unconnected with the business listed for discussion that day, and requiring urgent attention, 'namely, the revelations that a judge who was a witness in a recent murder trial had at a private court session approved an ex-parte application for the transfer of a liquor licence to the person who had been charged with the murder of her husband, had done so without giving the statutory notice to the Garda Síochána, and had breached the constitutional undertaking given by him.'

However, Seamus Patterson, the Ceann Comhairle, could not grant leave to move the motion. The Taoiseach, Mr Ahern, said: 'I understand my colleague, the Minister of Justice, Equality and Law Reform, has requested the president of the district court to investigate the matter and furnish a full report with all possible speed. He has also asked the garda commissioner for a report on the matter and he has asked the chief executive of the courts service to investigate these matters. . . . The minister must get the reports he has requested, at which time he will have no difficulty making a statement, the format of which can be agreed.'

The Minister of Justice added: 'The parties centrally involved in the matter were also centrally involved in different ways in an extremely serious criminal case, which was adjudicated upon on Tuesday of this week. There could be no question of formally conducting an in-depth examination of the kind now under way, and thereby running the risk of damaging the processing of the criminal proceedings.'

In my opinion, the Wicklow state solicitor should have appealed Judge O'Buachalla's decision to the Circuit Court. Personally, I was disappointed that they did not appeal; I would also have appreciated being informed of their views on the contents of my report. One has to wonder whether the matter would ever have come into the public domain had it not been for an article which appeared in *Magill* magazine on 13 April 2000.

The vexatious issue of the pub licence came before the House for debate on 18 April. Mr O'Donoghue informed the House that he was in possession of written reports from the garda commissioner and the CEO of the Courts Service. He also acknowledged that his department had had prior knowledge about the case, and said that he would deal with this when making a full statement on the matter. I cannot find evidence of any such statement from Mr O'Donoghue to Dáil Éireann, or to anyone else.

O'Donoghue then addressed the issue of the letters which had been sent to his department by the Nevin family. Two issues were raised by the Nevins, he said: first, whether it was lawful for the judge to act as he did; second, whether the judge had acted with propriety. His department's response pointed out that the judiciary is independent in the discharge of its responsibilities. It also stated that his department does not provide legal advice, and that it would be a matter for the person's lawyers to deal with that aspect of the matter.

Further correspondence had been received from the Nevins, he stated. Prior to replying, his department had contacted the office of the attorney general and was advised that counsel's opinion had been sought for the Gardaí by the chief state solicitor's office. A copy of that opinion was obtained by his department. He was reluctant to go into detail regarding the counsel's advice, lest it be construed that by doing so he was colouring Judge O'Buachalla's actions.

O'Donoghue's department did not become involved in the second issue raised: that is, the propriety of the actions taken by

O'Buachalla. He was aware of the major criminal trial which was about to take place, and the risk that public revelations about O'Buachalla would be deemed prejudicial to the trial.

Continuing, the minister stated: 'The president of the district court pointed out that the inquiry he has been asked to undertake is a very serious matter with grave implications. The president pointed out that when he met Judge O'Buachalla in connection with his inquiries, he was accompanied by senior counsel. Judge Smithwick felt he too would need to instruct a firm of solicitors, as well as senior counsel. . . . The only logical conclusion to draw from all this is that several issues will arise in the course of examining Judge O'Buachalla's role in connection with the licensing of Jack White's Inn, and these issues are far from straightforward. There have been suggestions that two members of the Garda Síochána were treated in an unfair manner in Judge O'Buachalla's court.'

The minister stated that the matters raised at that time had again been brought into the public domain, and would be looked at afresh. He informed the House that he would ask the chief justice to nominate a judge to conduct a formal, statutory-based inquiry into all aspects of the case. The judge appointed by the chief justice was Mr Justice Frank Murphy of the Supreme Court.

Of great relevance and importance was Minister O'Donoghue's statement that 'It is my firm intention to publish the reports in question.' This is a clear reference to the reports prepared and submitted by the garda commissioner, the CEO of the Courts Service, and the president of the district court.

Another promise in this regard by Minister O'Donoghoe made to the Dáil on 18 April 2000 was that 'The House and the public we represent are entitled to have the matters raised, and fully and properly investigated, without resort to prejudice, innuendo and other irrelevancies.'

Jim Higgins TD noted that there were some serious issues he wished to have clarified: 'The minster deliberately withheld from the Dáil the fact that he had received correspondence from the family of Tom Nevin, in which they expressed serious concerns about the issue of the pub licence granted to Catherine Nevin. The minister, through his secretary, replied to Mr Patsy Nevin on 19 April and 13 August 1999. In the correspondence, it was stated: "These applications were made in accordance with the rules governing same, due notice was given and they were all dealt with in open court." The Gardaí hotly dispute this, as is obvious from Inspector Finn's report and the very trenchant report from Superintendent Flynn. Did the information obtained from the court clerks, as mentioned by the Minister, confirm that correct procedures were followed? My understanding is that the district court clerks, particularly Mr Sexton in Arklow, were seriously unhappy with the procedures and that was the reason the hearing was transferred from Arklow to Wexford.'

Ruairí Quinn TD added: 'As far as I know, Section 21 [under which recommendations cannot be made, only findings reported] had not previously been invoked by a Minister of Justice. That in itself is an indication of the seriousness of the matter with which we are now dealing. Depending on the contents of the report furnished and then published by him, and presented for consideration to the House, this may become the first step in a process for removal by the Houses of the Oireachtas of a judge from office on the grounds of misbehaviour.'

The Sheedy case (a case of dangerous driving causing death, over which two judges resigned) was mentioned as having raised legitimate fears that all members of the public were not being treated equally before the law, and that those who had access to members of the judiciary were likely to be treated in a more favourable manner. 'Unless we get answers to the questions which arise in this case and the appropriate action is taken, if warranted, when the report is available, this perception will be reinforced.'

Higgins also stated: 'I assume that another document the minister had in his possession or was appraised of was the report on the proceedings, which he withheld from the Dáil, drawn up by Superintendent Flynn.'

O'Donoghue replied: 'A search conducted over the past few days found no evidence that two garda reports were forwarded to the department. We will continue to search, but on the face of it, there appears to be no reason the department would have sight of what was, after all, an internal garda document.'

These statements by the minister need to be looked at carefully. Presumably, the garda reports he referred to were those prepared by myself and Inspector Finn. These reports were not, as suggested by him, internal garda documents. I forwarded them to the local state solicitor, assuming that the opinions of the chief state solicitor and even the attorney general would be sought, if necessary. The Department of Justice is responsible for these offices.

Mr Higgins asked: 'Does the minister not accept, where there is a question mark and a major shadow, as there is here, Judge O'Buachalla would be doing a service to the judicial process, and public confidence in it, by standing aside in the short term until the matter is resolved, without any prejudice?'

Mr O'Donoghoe replied: 'I outlined that it was my intention to make a comprehensive statement when all the facts had been assembled and all the reports were available to me.'

I was struck by the differing aspects of the inquiry as set up by Mr O'Donoghue under Section 21 of the Courts of Justice (District Court) Act, 1946, and the tribunals. There are clearly defined powers given to the tribunal, which include making whatever broad recommendations it considers necessary or expedient. The clerk of the Dáil shall arrange to have any report from the tribunal laid before both Houses of the Oireachtas immediately on its receipt. Why were these powers not availed of in the O'Buachalla inquiry?

The inquiry into the granting of the pub licence to Catherine Nevin differed greatly in its terms of reference to those allowed/granted under the tribunals. The relevant portion of Section 21 allows a judge appointed by the Chief Justice 'to inquire into the conduct (whether in the execution of his office or otherwise) of a justice, either generally, or on a particular occasion'. On conclusion of the inquiry, the said judge shall report the result to the Minister of Justice.

The act is silent regarding any powers the judge may rely upon to do other than report the result of the inquiry to the minister. He and the Houses of the Oireachtas have powers to remove members of the judiciary from office if this is warranted.

The letter from the Department of Justice to the Nevin family stated: 'As the surviving joint licensee, Mrs Nevin was automatically entitled to be registered as the sole licensee and could simply apply under Section 16 of the Licensing Ireland Act, 1874, to be registered as the sole licensee and have the licence altered to reflect this change.' These views and opinions from the Department of Justice were given a year prior to the commencement of the inquiry by Judge Murphy.

The letter received by Patsy Nevin from the Department of Justice on 16 August 1999 stated: 'From inquiries made, I understand that the order pursuant to Section 16 of the Licensing Ireland Act, 1874, for the deleting of your brother's name from the licence attached to Jack White's Inn was made in Wexford District Court on 29 September 1997. I understand there was no formal written application before the court for such an order and that the order was not made in open court. In this regard, Section 16 of the Licensing Ireland Act is silent as to the formal and notice requirement of such an application.'

The act relied upon by O'Buachalla and Catherine's legal team is the Licensing Ireland Act, 1874, specifically section 16. This act was never mentioned by anyone at Wexford District Court. The verbiage used in this 134-year-old act is so at variance with modern and recent statute law as to be little short of comical. The reason it was used is simply because there is no later legislation they could rely on, or quote, to justify what was done at Wexford District Court on 29 September 1997.

The 1874 act cannot even be obtained from Irish Oifiguil, the government department one applies to for such acts. (They deal only with legislation passed after 1922.) To obtain legislation for the period prior to 1922, it was necessary to communicate with the equivalent UK office in Belfast. This I did, and obtained the relevant act.

Some references quoted hereunder indicate the intention to seek out any legislation which by its very nature, and ambiguous content, would, it is hoped, justify the procedure as adopted by Catherine Nevin's legal representatives, and Judge O'Buachalla. But even the legislation chosen by them does not justify what was done in Wexford in 1997.

Section 16 refers specifically to the Register of Licences to be kept in every petty sessions district. It also states and defines how, and to whom, a certificate for the grant, renewal or transfer of a licence may be made. It refers specifically to the requirement to produce a certificate dated earlier than the grant, transfer or renewal of a licence. It does not state that this section authorises the issue of a certificate, and in fact gives no power to issue anything.

Judge O'Buachalla, in a statement to the press on 13 April 2000, stated that he acted properly when he transferred the licence for Jack White's Inn into the name of Catherine Nevin. He also said that the application was made in open court.

However, addressing Inspector Peter Finn at Arklow District Court on 20 October 1997, after the pub licence had been granted by him, Judge O'Buachalla said: 'In reference to what went on at Wexford District Court on 29 September 1997, it is clear there was no transfer.'

On 13 April 2000, Judge O'Buachalla said: 'A renewal certificate cannot be granted to a dead person, and the licence had been in the joint names of Tom and Catherine Nevin. It became necessary to amend the existing licence so that a renewal could take place.' (This was later quoted in Judge Murphy's report.)

In my view, there is no power given under Section 16 of the act to amend the licence. Any such amendment as admitted to by Judge O'Buachalla is therefore not supported by Section 16.

I thought it would be a relatively easy task to secure the reports as commissioned by Justice Minister John O'Donoghue. Little did I realise the wondrous workings of the Department of Justice. The manner in which my efforts were dealt with speaks volumes for the office of the Minister for Justice, Equality and Law Reform.

My first letter to the Department of Justice requesting the reports was dated 26 June 2008. This went unanswered, and I sent two reminders in July 2008. Eventually, on 31 July, the following reply was received: 'I do not consider it appropriate to release the two reports. [The President of the District Court did not complete his report]. The then-minister made no undertaking to make the reports available to others, nor did he imply that he would do so. On 13 April 2000, the minister told the Dáil: 'I will examine the three reports when they are to hand, and I will make a full statement on the matter at the earliest possible date.' (This indicates that the reports were prepared on a confidential basis for his information prior to making a full statement). Consequently, I must regretfully decline to release the reports as requested.' Signed: Oonagh McPhilips, Courts Policy Division.

An acknowledgement of the letter's receipt, also dated 31 July 2008, was sent to me, signed 'Barry O'Donnell, Private Secretary'. I sent another letter to the secretary, dated 27 August, and a separate letter to Oonagh McPhilips. Commenting on the contents of her reply, I wrote: 'I do not regard myself as "others", rather as the one who put the issue into the public domain. Am I to assume that, as the writer and instigator of the report, which resulted in the matter being debated in Dáil Éireann, and as a result of which three separate inquiries were set up by the Minister of Justice, that I am to remain ignorant as to the outcome of them? Presumably not! Should you so hold, then it stands to reason that the public are also to remain ignorant of the outcome – an outcome all concerned persons are entitled to have put at their disposal.'

Duplication led to serious confusion within the Department of Justice, as a second reply to the same letter was sent by Oonagh McPhilips, Courts Policy Division, dated 22 September 2008. She wrote: 'I am sure you will understand that the department corresponds with the Gardaí through the Commissioner of an Garda Síochána and it is not possible to release confidential material to retired members. As outlined in my previous reply of 31 July 2008, no undertaking was given to make these reports public. In the circumstances, I regret that this department cannot be of further assistance to you in this matter.'

Another reply came from one Cunningham, Private Secretary, dated 25 September 2008: 'I am directed by the Minister of Justice, Equality and Law Reform to refer to your letter of 27 August 2008, seeking copies of three reports to the then Minister in Dáil Éireann, in April 2000. I understand the relevant line division had replied to you directly. In the circumstances I regret that I can be of no further assistance to you in this matter.'

This had now become, because of the manner in which I was being treated by the Department of Justice, an issue I was determined to pursue to the bitter end. I wondered why Oonagh McPhilips had said: 'No undertaking was given to make these reports public.' I was becoming concerned about what was being concealed not just from myself, but also from the public at large. If there was nothing explosive or damning in the reports, why the secrecy? Catherine Nevin is incarcerated in prison, for life. Justice was done, and seen to be done, when she was convicted of murder, but she left unfinished business in her wake.

I wrote again on 4 October 2008 to the Private Secretary, referring to Ms McPhilips's statement that 'No undertaking was given to make these reports public.' I asked: 'At what stage, or by whom, was the information sought by me deemed to be confidential? . . . In fact, Mr O'Donoghue, in his address to the Dáil, and replies to questions, gave certain undertakings, one of which included a promise to publish and make public the reports.'

My letter continues: 'Mr O'Donoghue also informed the House he was in possession of written reports from the Garda Commissioner, and the Chief Executive of the Courts Service, and that he would make a comprehensive statement when all the facts had been assembled. I now ask for a copy of that statement. If you will not supply it, then please confirm or deny he made the statement in Dáil Éireann. . . . Another undertaking given by Mr O'Donoghue TD, on 18 April 2000, to the Dáil: "It is my firm intention to publish the reports in question." . . . Please indicate if the then Minister of Justice, Mr John O'Donoghue, honoured that promise. If such reports were published, please be good enough to supply me with copies.' Just what can of worms had the inquiries opened, which changed the attitude of the Department of Justice to such an extent that they were apparently not prepared to honour commitments given by Justice Minister John O'Donoghue?

My most recent letter was not replied to, and I sent a reminder, asking for a reply by return of post. I was not even sure if the contents of my many letters had been brought to the attention of the then minister, Dermot Ahern. To be certain, I decided to make one last attempt to secure copies of the reports. I sent copies of all correspondence by registered letter, marked 'Personal and Confidential', to Mr Ahern on 5 January 2009. I also sent a copy by email and post to the private secretary. I decided that this would be the last communication I would have with the Department of Justice on the matter.

On 3 April 2009, the long-awaited reply arrived from Barry O'Donnell, Private Secretary, as directed by Mr Dermot Ahern, Minister of Justice, Equality and Law Reform. The letter, dated 20 March, stated: 'As previously advised to you, the reports to which you refer were prepared for the then minister on a confidential basis and no undertaking was given to make the reports public. During an Adjournment Debate in Dáil Éireann on 13 April 2000 on this matter, the then minister made reference to the reports he had requested from a number of individuals. He also gave an undertaking to provide a more comprehensive statement when all the facts were assembled.

'Minister O'Donoghue issued a more comprehensive statement on 18 April 2000 when he announced that he would ask the Chief Justice, in accordance with Section 21 of the Courts of Justice (District Court) Act, 1946, to nominate a judge to conduct a formal statutory-based inquiry into all aspects of this matter. As you know, the Hon. Mr Justice Frank Murphy, a judge of the Supreme Court, was appointed to conduct the inquiry.

'The then-minister stated at the time: "The situation is that Mr Justice Murphy will take over the inquiry and will become the investigating judge. All other inquiries which have commenced will cease and, in so far as they were completed, will be furnished to the High Court judge." The judge completed his inquiry and his report was published in full. In the circumstances, the minister regrets that he cannot be of any further assistance to you on this matter.'

37

Inquiry by Judge Frank Murphy

On 18 April 2000, Mr Frank D. Murphy, judge of the Supreme Court, was appointed 'to inquire into the conduct of District Judge Donnacha O'Buachalla in relation to the propriety of his handling of the licensing of the premises known as Jack White's Inn, having regard to his acquaintance with its licensee, Mrs Catherine Nevin, and in relation to the discharge of his judicial functions in cases involving two Gardaí against whom complaints had been made by Mrs Catherine Nevin.' His completed report was forwarded to the minister for justice on 23 November 2000.

Before going any further, it is necessary to indicate the position in relation to the pub licence between 19 March 1996, the date Tom Nevin was murdered, and 29 September 1997, the date that the unlisted application to move the licence into the sole name of Catherine Nevin was successful at Wexford District Court. The licence was held jointly in the name of Tom and Catherine Nevin and remained so until 30 September 1996. The licence was due to expire on 30 September 1996 and should have been renewed at Arklow annual licensing court in September 1996. The only applications made for Jack White's Inn were in respect of the ancillary licences, and those were granted at Arklow Court on 16

September 1996. Catherine had then not been charged with the murder of her husband, and there was no reason for any garda objections to the application. The pub licence could still be renewed up to 30 September 1996. As a result, there was effectively no licence in force from 1 October 1996.

Between 1 October 1996 and 29 September 1997, Catherine Nevin's legal team made frantic efforts to get the licence into her sole name. She then stood charged with the murder of Tom Nevin. It should also be pointed out that the licence remained in force for just one day, 30 September 1997. The objective of having the licence put into the sole name of Catherine Nevin had been achieved, and any renewal of it thereafter should be routine.

Mr Lehane, Catherine's solicitor, met with Judge O'Buachalla and Liam Sexton at Gorey Courthouse on 13 June 1997. Mr Lehane referred to the refusal of the Revenue Commissioners to renew the licence without an order of the court. The judge canvassed Mr Sexton's views on the issue as to whether a court order was necessary: he was emphatic that it was.

At the inquiry, Mr Lehane gave evidence that he had spoken to a Mr Goodwin at the Collectors Office in Waterford. Mr Lehane proposed that 'if we got an authorisation from the judge to delete Mr Nevin's name, would they accept that? Mr Lehane's recollection was that an authorisation, as he understood it, following his conversation with Mr Goodwin, might – might – meet requirements.' Mr Goodwin's recollection was different. He maintained the view that the Revenue would require an order of the court transferring the licence to Mrs Nevin before a renewal could issue.

The matter was submitted to Etain Croasdell, the assistant Revenue solicitor. Her view was that there should be a court transfer. She also stated: 'If there is any change in the identity of the licence holder, a court certificate is necessary, even if the change is the deletion of one party to the licence.'

Mr Lehane responded that Judge O'Buachalla had signed a letter of authorisation, which was enclosed with his letter. Ms

Croasdell pointed out that this was not a court order. Mr Goodwin wrote to Mr Sexton and asked: 'Is the authorisation signed by Judge O'Buachalla, dated 13 June 1997, an order of the court, and if so, was the order made by the judge in open court? If so, was the superintendent at Gorey under notice regarding the hearing? If the superintendent was in court, what was his attitude?' Judge O'Buachalla promptly confirmed that 'the letter of authorisation was not an order of the court'. The Gardaí informed Mr Lehane that they would be objecting to the applications for the ancillary licences, as there was not a current licence in force to which the ancillary licences could be subsidiary.

Judge Murphy's report continues: 'At Wexford District Court on 29 September 1997, when the judge arrived and entered his chambers, Mr Andy Cullen, the court clerk, and Ms Olive Stewart, a court official, were already there. Mr Lehane and Mr O'Toole, barrister for Catherine Nevin, were invited to his chambers, and the judge told Mr Cullen to call Inspector Finn to his chambers also. Inspector Finn informed all present that the Gardaí had not received notice of any application pertaining to the pub licence at Jack White's. Mr O'Toole stated it was an ex-parte application. The Inspector quite rightly suggested he should withdraw, as he was not party to the matter, but Judge O'Buachalla asked him to remain.'

Mr Cullen was deeply concerned about the propriety of the proceedings. He stated: 'I have never come across such an application being dealt with in that fashion in thirty-seven years as a court clerk.' Judge O'Buachalla asked everybody except Mr Cullen to leave. A lapse of two or three minutes passed before all parties were called back to the judge's chambers. In the interim, Mr Cullen had changed his stance on the issue.

Judge Murphy's report states: 'Mr Cullen became convinced he was mistaken. He had understood that the application being made was for the transfer by the judge of a publican's licence, and it was that to which he objected. He was now satisfied that it was an application to regularise the licence, and the judge did have jurisdiction to grant it.'

Inspector Finn was supplied with a copy of the order being sought. Speaking to him on the phone later, I told him that as it was an ex-parte application, the Gardaí, and he as their representative, had no function in the matter. 'Ms Croasdell, for the Revenue, informed Finn that they would accept the wording of the order. On 29 September 1997, the Customs and Excise office in Waterford issued the publican's licence to Mrs Nevin in her sole name for the year ended 30 September 1997. On 17 October 1997, a renewal of it was issued in her sole name for the year ending 30 September 1998.'

On 20 October 1997, Judge O'Buachalla granted two of the three ancillary licences at Arklow District Court. Judge O' Buachalla said: 'It is clear there was no transfer of this licence, it was only a renewal. The only matter now outstanding is the early-morning licence. Is that correct, Inspector?' The Inspector agreed. There was a garda objection in respect of the General Exemption Order, and it was adjourned to 24 November 1997.

When the adjourned application came before the court in Arklow, I represented the Gardaí, and Judge Connellan was the presiding judge. After much argument, the application was refused. Catherine gave evidence and I cross-examined her. I saw this as a golden opportunity to put her under pressure and to see how she would react to cross-examination.

In her direct evidence, she insisted that the General Exemption Order was necessary to cope with the ever-increasing volume of traffic, especially trucks, using the N11 route to Rosslare. There was also the proposed building of a factory a few miles from the pub. She wished to cater for these hard-working people before normal pub opening hours. Nothing whatever to do with boosting the sales of liquor?' she was asked. 'No, my lord, certainly not.'

Not long into cross-examination, my presence and questions

were having the desired effect. If she wanted her application to be successful, it required some limited degree of civility from her. This was too high a price to pay for her. Before long, she lost her cool and started throwing questions at me. She had evidently forgotten that, in this setting, she was not the star of the show – a fact that was politely impressed upon her. The judge wasn't impressed and the application was duly dismissed.

Referring to myself in his report, Judge Murphy states: 'The Superintendent was concerned, indeed more than that he was appalled by the order Judge O'Buachalla had made at Wexford District Court on 29 September. Like the majority of those who were called upon to form a view on the matter, he believed the appropriate procedure for the registration of Mrs Nevin as the sole licensee, was an ad interim transfer, followed by a confirmation of transfer. The Superintendent brought to his judgement a very considerable expertise. He had some thirty-five years' experience dealing with the enforcement of the Intoxicating Liquor Acts. The two points particularly stressed by the Superintendent were, first, as Superintendent for the area he was not given notice of the application to transfer the licence, and secondly that the application on 29 September was heard in the privacy of the judge's chambers.'

The advice of Mr Thomas M. Morgan, barrister, regarded as an expert on the Licensing Laws, was obtained by the State Solicitor. Morgan came down firmly against the transfer procedure. In circumstances such as Catherine Nevin found herself after the death of her husband, he held that the survivor would simply move an ex-parte application to the District Court, with the survivor's sole name as licence holder being substituted as a correction in the Licensing Register – as a result of which a court order made pursuant to Section 16 of the 1874 Act should permit the Revenue Commissioners to overcome any difficulties they may otherwise have had.

Morgan further stated that no objection to the renewal, which was held in public, was made in September 1996. He continues: 'There is no evidence and no suggestion whatsoever that any element of capriciousness or wrongdoing can or should be ascribed or attached to the District Court Judge in making the mistake of dealing with the technicality in chambers.'

Judge Murphy states in his report: 'Accordingly, the opinion of Mr Morgan resolved the conflict between Mr Lehane and the Revenue Authorities firmly in favour of Mr Lehane and specifically upheld the jurisdiction of the judge to grant the relief sought on 29 September 1997.'

I dispute Mr Morgan's opinions, as there was no application before the court and there was never a public hearing anywhere, or on any date, in respect of this issue.

Judge Murphy referred to Judge O'Buachalla's statement to the media on 13 April, 2000, which said: 'A renewal certificate cannot be granted to a dead person, and the licence had been in the joint names of Tom and Catherine Nevin. This difficulty was brought to the attention of the courts in September 1997, and Inspector Finn, Gorey, attended all the discussions in relation to the matter to amend the licence so that a renewal could take place. There was no objection by the Gardaí at the Annual Licensing Court to renewal of the licence in the sole name of Catherine Nevin.'

Judge Murphy concluded: 'That statement was both inaccurate and incomplete. It was clearly wrong to say the application was made in open court. It was not. It was held in the judge's chambers in the District Court in Wexford. Again, Inspector Finn did not attend the meeting held in the judge's chambers in Gorey on 13 June 1997. The statement is either incomplete in not extending to that meeting or is inaccurate in implying that Inspector Finn was present at it. In fact the statement may have focused further attention on the judge. The fact that he was acquainted with Mrs Nevin; that he made an order in his judicial capacity which appeared to confer a benefit on her; and that it emerged that one application had been heard in chambers, may well have given rise to the suspicion that an abuse of the legal process had occurred. I am satisfied that the undisputed facts of the case do not support such an inference or justify such a suspicion.'

Judge Murphy said: 'The hearing of the application was in my opinion undesirable and the judge is open to criticism for doing so. I believe that the failure to disqualify himself from hearing the application in Wexford on 29 September 1997 was an error of judgement and not of misconduct.

'It was proper for the judge on 13 June 1997 to listen to Mr Lehane's account of the problems which he had encountered in renewing the licence in the sole name of Catherine Nevin . . . The judge suggested Mr Lehane should contact the Collector of Customs & Excise at Waterford, and this could hardly be criticised, but the fact that it was reported back to the judge that the Revenue needed or wanted some form of document from the judge to overcome the difficulty in renewing the licence appears to have encouraged the judge to intervene in a manner which can be seen, certainly with the benefit of hindsight, to have been undesirable . . . Judge O'Buachalla had no power to issue the letter of authorisation, and accordingly he should not have done so. In particular it is regrettable that the letter was issued in a form which might suggest that it was an order of the court rather than a letter of comfort. The only disagreement between every lawyer and official concerned was the procedure by which the licence would be obtained, and many disagreed vehemently. It was this procedural difficulty the judge was invited to resolve by issuing a letter of authorisation. In my view he erred in acceding to that request but this was an error of judgement, and not an abuse of the legal process.

'The fact that the application was dealt with behind closed doors could in any case, and did in the present, give rise to a suspicion that some wrongdoing was being perpetrated. Such a suspicion could be damaging to the administration of justice and was,

I am afraid, damaging to the reputation of the judge involved . . . It is an oversight which he has every reason to regret.'

These comments by Judge Murphy are damning and far-reaching. I still point the finger of suspicion at the entire procedure. My report that the procedure was without precedent in law, and unlawful, remains my opinion.

Concluding, Judge Murphy stated: 'I have requested that Mr Buckley, Solicitor to the Inquiry, do deliver to the Department of Justice, Equality and Law Reform, material documentation produced to me in relation to the inquiry so that it may be retained in the archives of the Department or to be disposed of as the Minister thinks fit.' The material documentation includes the three reports refused to me.

The second part of Judge Murphy's report deals with the complaints of Gardaí Vincent Whelan and Michael Murphy against Judge Donnacha O'Buachalla, arising out of their appearances in the District Court when he was the presiding judge. They felt they were being treated unfairly by him – and differently from the way the other Gardaí were being treated. This, they believed, was because of the judge's friendship with Catherine Nevin, and the many complaints she had made against them. The media got hold of the complaints made by Murphy and Whelan, and as a result there was huge coverage and interest in the story.

I had regular contact with Gardaí Murphy and Whelan leading up to the day their complaints would get a hearing before Judge Frank Murphy. There was no indication that there were to be any sensational developments. Judge Murphy had taken up his position, and Mr McGonigle SC, representing the Gardaí, rose to address him. There was complete silence as Mr McGonigle started what everyone assumed would be his opening salvo.

'Your Honour, I wish to inform you that the Gardaí . . . are satisfied that there is no basis for making any complaint against District Justice O'Buachalla in respect of any of the dates [which are] the subject matter of this inquiry, or, indeed any other dates.

We formally withdraw the complaints, such as they are. We are sat-isfied that everything which District Justice O'Buachalla did on those occasions was done within jurisdiction and so far as they are concerned, no stain or blemish should attach to Justice O'Buachalla.'

There was stunned silence as the U-turn by Gardaí Murphy and Whelan was announced. The assembled reporters stared in disbelief at both Gardaí, who had effectively robbed them of front-page stories. I was also shocked. I had listened to their tales of woe concerning their alleged treatment by Judge O'Buachalla. They had made their complaints to, and had the backing of, the Garda Representative Association, and had their grievances aired in Dáil Éireann. I have great difficulty in understanding the logic behind them making such potentially dangerous allegations against a judge and, when being given the opportunity to substan-tiate them, declining to do so.

Judge Murphy's report was sent to Mr O'Donoghue TD on 23 November 2000. Mr O'Donoghue was aware that the presiding judge did not have any specific powers to make any recommenda-tions on conclusion of his inquiry and report. Did Judge Murphy's report contain anything that the minister felt should be addressed by him and the Houses of the Oireachtas?

The acknowledgement by Judge Murphy that article 34.1 of the Constitution had not been complied with when the application for the pub licence was made should have alarmed the minister. Did he notice Judge Murphy's many condemnations of the behav-ior of Judge O'Buachalla in relation to the entire unsavoury pro-cedure? If he did, then his silence is deafening. Perhaps Mr O'Donoghue accepts that no wrongdoing was perpetrated, and as a result no comment or publicity was required. Even had he so decided, there still remained his unfulfilled promises to publish the reports. Why did the Department of Justice repeatedly refuse to supply me with the reports I had been seeking?

Without the cooperation of the present Minister of Justice,

Mr Dermot Ahern, the content of those reports will remain the sole preserve of the Department of Justice. In this case, not only will the administration of justice in this country continue to be viewed by the masses as selective, especially towards those holding office of power or influence, but it will also continue to be viewed as favouring one sector of society over the other, thus giving a clear indication that the administration of justice can be, and often is, tainted.

Mr Jim Higgins TD stated on 13 April 2000 in Dáil Éireann: 'This judicial episode taints once again the administration of justice. The courts are the cornerstone of the Constitution and our democracy. Judges must be above suspicion. They must be people of integrity, substance and character. There must not be question marks over their character.'

The government retain certain powers in relation to questionable activities by members of the judiciary. They must of course have the courage to use these powers if and when necessary.

I brought the conduct of Judge O'Buachalla when granting the pub licence to the attention of the Law Officers and Garda Headquarters. Perhaps I should have awakened the sleeping dogs before I did, but they are now fully awake, and anxious for a return to a more justified, dignified and peaceful slumber.

38

CONCLUSION

In hindsight, the murder of Tom Nevin on 19 March 1996 and what transpired thereafter could not, and possibly never will be, surpassed in Irish legal history. Many lives were shattered, some beyond repair. Noted personalities, not least of whom are Judge Donnacha O'Buachalla and former garda inspector Tom Kennedy, got caught up in the investigation for various reasons.

On 16 October 2006, the family of Tom Nevin commenced legal proceedings to stop Catherine from collecting rent on two properties which had been jointly owned by Tom and her. The claim is retrospective to the date of Tom's murder.

The pub was sold shortly before Christmas 1997 for £620,000. Ownership of that money is being contested by the Nevin family. It is estimated conservatively that the rental properties are worth in excess of €800,000 collectively. The properties, plus the insurance policies on Tom Nevin's life, will make Catherine a very wealthy woman on her release, if the action being brought by Patsy Nevin and his sister, Margaret Lavelle, is unsuccessful. The Nevins are determined to pursue every legal avenue open to them to ensure that Catherine never benefits as a result of the murder of her husband.

Catherine's last appeal was in the Court of Criminal Appeal on 3 April 2009. She attempted to have her conviction for the murder of her husband Tom Nevin declared a miscarriage of justice. Catherine was applying for an order forcing the Director of Public Prosecutions to answer whether or not the three main witnesses, William McClean, John Jones and Gerard Heapes, were ever state informers, and whether McClean had paramilitary connections. The application was again adjourned on that date.

Having failed to have her conviction overturned, Catherine and her legal team had one final throw of the dice left. This centred on the claim that state witnesses Gerry Heapes and John Jones were state informers and that a third, William McClean, had paramilitary connections. All three had claimed at Mrs Nevin's trial that they had been solicited by her to kill her husband; all had stated under oath that they had refused to do so. Her legal team had some success in this legal confrontation relating to the release of secret Garda secret files. The state, for obvious reasons, contested the application. Catherine's legal team alleged that the documents would show that Heapes and Jones, were suspects in the case and that a file on McClean lists members of the INLA and Provisional IRA as associates of him. McClean denied at all times, including during the trial, that he had any such links.

Hugh Hartnett SC told the appeal court in July 2010 that the newly discovered facts proved that the men responsible for putting their client behind bars had every reason to collude and tell lies. Mr Hartnett added that the files showed that the witness had strong paramilitary connections which, if disclosed, could have swayed the jury in Mrs Nevin's favour.

The court intimated that it would deliver its decision 'soon'. The judgment was eagerly awaited, and attracted much media attention. In an article published on 22 November 2010, the *Irish Daily Mail* ran the following headline: 'BLACK WIDOW' COULD SUE FOR €10 MILLION IF SHE IS FREED TODAY. The previous day, the same newspaper, in an article headlined 'BLACK WIDOW' HOPING

TO BE OUT TOMORROW AS JUDGES RULE ON HER APPEAL, suggested that 'there are growing concerns among legal circles and Garda circles that her controversial conviction could be declared unsafe and she will walk free'.

The Court of Criminal Appeal delivered its decision on 22 November 2010. The court was emphatic when stating, in reference to the Garda forms: 'None of the forms in question is, in and of itself, of any evidential effect: that is to say, they prove nothing. Information contained in them is often clearly hearsay or opinion. In the course of the trial, the learned trial judge indicated that disclosure should be limited to facts which are relevant to the issues in the trial and did not intend to opinion or speculation. That was a perfectly proper approach, and very necessary for the protection of people who might have a very tenuous or innocent association with a person who would come to Garda attention. The fact is that the 'suspect antecedent history form' simply does not live up to its billing. It is not a form relating to suspects despite its title, and this is clearly demonstrated by the fact that such a form had been filled out in respect of people who are clearly not suspects.

The decision continues: 'The court finds not the least support for the claims made in relation to the documents, which it has examined', and notes what was said by the Court of Criminal Appeal in the applicant's appeal against her conviction: 'This court has carefully and thoroughly examined each file in question and is completely satisfied that there is nothing contained therein that could in any way have assisted the applicant's defence either directly or indirectly or by leading to other information that might be of assistance in that regard. Therefore, there is no basis for making any order of disclosure, as sought.' They, the judges, also agreed with the statement of the learned trial judge when rejecting the application for disclosure of the documents because of lack of relevancy. Addressing the credibility of the three men, it said that none of them were put forward at the trial as being persons of good character. It is a well-established fact appreciated by most police forces that anyone seeking to employ the services of an assassin would be slow to approach a person or persons of unblemished character. It also found that Nevin's case was 'in certain important particulars, very vague'.

The final paragraph of the judgement could hardly be more explicit: 'The learned trial judge, at the conclusion of the trial, expressed her view that the applicant here had her husband assassinated and had then attempted to assassinate his character. This court reiterates these views. This case is dismissed.'

Catherine Nevin has featured regularly in the newspapers in recent years, recently in connection with illegal possession of mobile phones, and in an article suggesting that she will be suing the state for in excess of €9.5 million if her appeal is successful.

It has been revealed by fellow inmates that she is seeking to sell her true story for in excess of €1 million. It has been suggested that she is getting assistance in writing a book.

Life has brought many changes to some of those directly or indirectly involved in the investigation.

> The Nevin family still await finality to the civil action entered by them concerning their dead brother's properties – all of which Catherine is claiming, despite being convicted of the murder of the co-owner.

> I retired in 2004 and moved to an idyllic home and setting in County Wexford.

> Detective Joe Collins retired in 2006, and is anxiously trying to lower his golf handicap.

> Detective Sergeant Fergus O'Brien is still serving with distinction in An Garda Síochána, as are Detectives Pat Mulcahy, Paul Commiskey and Aubrey Steedman.

> Detective Gerry McKenna is retired and is also spending a lot of his time improving his golf.

Sergeant Joe O'Hara (now Detective Sergeant) and Sergeant Brian Duffy have been relocated to the Dublin Metropolitan Area.

Detective Tom Byrne is retired since 2002, and is devoting most of his time to promoting underage hurling in County Wicklow. His good friend Detective Bernie Hanly is still serving in Dublin.

Detective Jim McCawl ('the Equaliser') retired in 2003 – much to Catherine's delight.

Detective Superintendent McElligott is retired.

Garda Paul Cummiskey was appointed to, and is still serving in, Detective Branch at Arklow.

Assistant Commissioner J. McHugh is retired.

Detective Sergeant Liam Hogan is now a superintendent serving in the Dublin area. He is deserving of a much higher rank.

Former garda inspector Tom Kennedy is still living in Wicklow town.

Judge Donnacha O'Buachalla is still the resident Judge for District Court Area Number 23.

Catherine still uses her marriage name 'Nevin', despite being convicted of murdering the man from whom she received it. Information emanating from prison suggests that she has changed little in prison. Early in her incarceration, she sought out the person whom she believed to be the big boss of her fellow inmates, and temporarily gained the confidence (or so she believed) of a person much further down the pecking order, none other than Ms Felloni, a well-known member of a well-known family.

If Catherine intends writing a true factual account of Tom's murder, it will, like all her other evil acts, be motivated by the one true love of her life: money. No doubt her true story would be a best-seller, but would she ever get to enjoy the financial harvest the proceeds could throw up? Her hoped-for overturn of her convictions would also have serious consequences for her book. She could not rely on telling the true story of the murder, as she would be an innocent woman cleared of any involvement in it.

Life in prison has been reasonably kind to Catherine. Her continued detention is some small comfort for the Nevin family, and the members of the Gardaí who worked so tirelessly to put her where she undoubtedly deserves to be, and hopefully will remain for the duration of the sentence she received: *life*.